Aunt Bee's
Mealtime in Mayberry

Aunt Bee's Mealtime in Mayberry

Recipes and Memories from America's Friendliest Town

KEN BECK AND JIM CLARK

RUTLEDGE HILL PRESS®

Nashville, Tennessee

Published in Nashville, Tennessee, by Rutledge Hill Press®, 211 Seventh Avenue North, Nashville, Tennessee 37219.

Distributed in Canada by H. B. Fenn & Company, Ltd., 34 Nixon Road, Bolton, Ontario L7E 1W2.

Distributed in Australia by The Five Mile Press Pty., Ltd., 22 Summit Road, Noble Park, Victoria 3174.

Distributed in New Zealand by Southern Publishers Group, 22 Burleigh Street, Grafton, Auckland, New Zealand.

Distributed in the United Kingdom by Verulam Publishing, Ltd., 152a Park Street Lane, Park Street, St. Albans, Hertfordshire AL2 2AU.

Typography by Roger A. DeLiso, Rutledge Hill Press®

Design by Harriette Bateman, Bateman Design

Library of Congress Cataloging-in-Publication Data

Clark, Jim, 1960–
    Aunt Bee's mealtime in Mayberry / by Jim Clark and Ken Beck.
      p.   cm.
    Includes index.
    ISBN 1-55853-737-6
    1. Cookery.   2. Andy Griffith show (Television program)   I. Beck, Ken, 1951– . II.
    Title.
TX714.C553 1999   98-55326
641.5—dc21   CIP

Printed in the United States of America

1 2 3 4 5 6 7 8 9—02 01 00 99

Dedicated to the cast,

production crew, and writers of

The Andy Griffith Show

Quotations from *The Andy Griffith Show* used in this book are from the following episodes and these writers: "The New Housekeeper," "The Guitar Player," "Ellie Comes to Town," "Ellie for Council," "Alcohol and Old Lace," "Aunt Bee the Warden," and "Three's a Crowd" by **Jack Elinson and Charles Stewart**; "The Cannon" and "Aunt Bee Learns to Drive," by **Jack Elinson**; "Andy the Matchmaker" by **Arthur Stander**; "Christmas Story," "Andy and Opie, Housekeepers," and "Opie and the Bully" by **David Adler**; "Aunt Bee's Brief Encounter" and "Bailey's Bad Boy" by **Ben Gershman and Leo Solomon**; "The Clubmen" by **Fred S. Fox and Iz Elinson**; "The Pickle Story," "Andy and Barney in the Big City," "Wedding Bells for Aunt Bee," "The Bed Jacket," "The Loaded Goat," "Andy's English Valet," "The Big House," "Barney and the Cave Rescue," "The Return of Malcolm Merriweather," "Back to Nature," "The Pageant" and "Malcolm at the Crossroads," by **Harvey Bullock**; "Cousin Virgil" by **Phillip Shuken and Johnny Greene**; "Opie's Rival" by **Sid Morse**; "Andy and Opie, Bachelors," "Convicts at Large," "Man in a Hurry," "Class Reunion," "The Darlings Are Coming," "Dogs, Dogs, Dogs," "Briscoe Declares for Aunt Bee," "Gomer the House Guest," "Ernest T. Bass Joins the Army," "Up in Barney's Room," "My Fair Ernest T. Bass," and "Family Visit" by **Jim Fritzell and Everett Greenbaum**; "Aunt Bee's Medicine Man," "The Sermon for Today," "Opie's Ill-Gotten Gain," "Opie and His Merry Men," and "Bargain Day" by **John Whedon**; "A Wife for Andy" and "Barney Hosts a Summit Meeting" by **Aaron Ruben**; "Barney and Thelma Lou, Phffft," "Big Fish in a Small Town," and "Andy and Helen Have Their Day" by **Bill Idelson and Sam Bobrick**; "Barney's Physical" and "Banjo-Playing Deputy" by **Bob Ross**; "Guest in the House" and "A Warning from Warren" by **Fred Freeman and Lawrence J. Cohen**; "The Arrest of the Fun Girls" by **Richard M. Powell**; "The Bazaar" and "Eat Your Heart Out" by **Ben Joelson and Art Baer**; "The Gypsies" by **Roland MacLane**; "A Singer in Town" by **Stan Dreben and Howard Merrill**; "The Darling Fortune" by **Jim Parker and Arnold Margolin**; "A New Doctor in Town" by **Ray Brenner and Barry Blitzer**; "Dinner at Eight" by **Budd Grossman**; "Aunt Bee's Restaurant" by **Ronald Axe and Les Roberts**; "Howard's Main Event" and "The Church Benefactors" by **Robert C. Dennis and Earl Barret**; "Opie Steps Up in Class," "Howard and Millie," and "The Wedding" by **Joe Bonaduce**; "Helen, the Authoress" by **Doug Tibbles**; "Goodbye Dolly" and "Aunt Bee and the Lecturer" by **Michael Morris and Seaman Jacobs**; "Howard's New Life" and "Sam for Town Council" by **Dick Bensfield and Perry Grant**; and "Emmett's Brother-in-Law" and "The Mayberry Chef" by **James L. Brooks**.

TRAY BIEN, GARÇON—*"Sandy" Taylor has his apron strings tied pretty tight as he caters to budding author Helene Alexion DuBois. Even so, no one appreciates talented writers more than Andy does.*

Contents

Episodes

Recipes

Acknowledgments

As always, we've had a great deal of help and support from our friends and families in writing and compiling this book. For most of the recipes, we tapped into our families' deep recipe files, which lean heavily on Southern cooking. Our heartfelt thanks go to Ken's wife, Wendy, and Jim's wife, Mary, for their help with the recipes and with every other aspect of this book and, for that matter, our lives!

Ken also thanks his daughter, Kylie, and his son, Cole. And neither of us would have become hearty eaters without the good cooking of our mothers, Hazel Beck and Nancy Clark, both of whom have given us recipes used in this book.

We also have included recipes shared with us by Sherry Hyatt, Janine Johnson, Anna Dale, Gail Baddeley, Wayne Baddeley, Lisa Baldwin, Jo Palmer Beard, Corinne Bain, Cindy Beck, Betty Burroughs, Barbara Midgett Davis, Linda Ezzell, Ray Ezzell, Sheila Farris, Evelyn Gailbreath, Irene Inman, Debbie Johnson, James Earl Keel, Jewell Leonard, Carol Locke, Tammy Lee, Gertie LeCornu, Helen Martin, Mara Butler, Alice Jarman Penuel, Anita Pruitt, Connie Prosser, Marcia Ray, Donneita Rogers, Brenda Harvell Smith, Lynda Ann Sparkman, Tina Muncy, Sherry Beck, and Melody Ward.

While recipes are surely the main course of any cookbook, a Mayberry cookbook wouldn't be Mayberry at all without the magic produced by Andy Griffith and all of the cast, crew, and writers who made *The Andy Griffith Show*. They are the ones who created the characters and stories that we have loved for the last four decades and will continue to enjoy for many decades to come. Simply to say thank you to them hardly seems adequate.

That's why once again this cookbook is being dedicated to the cast, production crew, and writers. We hope that this book will serve as at least a small homage to their extraordinary achievements in making *The Andy Griffith Show*. This cookbook is merely a reflection—and just a glimpse at that—of their brilliant work, which surely will continue to shine for as long as audiences appreciate inspired performances, superb storytelling, and unsurpassed entertainment.

We're grateful to Mayberry Enterprises and Viacom Consumer Products for letting us compile this book, and particularly to Tim Gaskill, Viacom's supervisor of publishing, for his special assistance with photographs and with other matters. We also thank publisher Larry Stone at Rutledge Hill Press for once again indulging two Goobers in the kitchen. In addition, we thank editor Geoff Stone, recipe editor Laurin Stamm, marketing man Bryan Curtis, publicist Stacie Kutzbach, designer Harriette Bateman, typographer Roger DeLiso, and all of the staff at Rutledge Hill Press.

Thank you all. You beat everything, you know that!

—Ken Beck and Jim Clark

MEALTIME IN MAYBERRY—*A meal that's Taylor made suits everybody in Mayberry just fine.*

Introduction

This book was born out of a real appetite for Mayberry. We had a lot of fun with our first cookbook, *Aunt Bee's Mayberry Cookbook*, which was published by Rutledge Hill Press in 1991. It is a complete cookbook with a full range of recipes and menus contributed both by fans and by members of the show's cast, crew, and team of writers.

Our second cookbook tribute to Mayberry, *Aunt Bee's Delightful Desserts*, published in 1996, follows the same pattern, but with even more widespread participation by the show's regular cast, crew, writers, and guest stars.

Between the two cookbooks, both of which contain hundreds of recipes and lots of Mayberry photographs, dialogue, and trivia, we felt we had pretty well covered the culinary aspects of Mayberry. But we began scratching our heads (and patting our bellies) and pondering if there was something else that we could bring to the Mayberry dinner table. After all, we still enjoy eating as much as ever and there's no subject we'd rather write about more than Mayberry.

So, we began thinking. What if we could compile a cookbook with color as well as black-and-white photographs? That would add an attractive new dimension. And what if we could show some images that had never before been seen except in the episodes themselves? That would be really neat. If many of those photographs depicted actual scenes of food being prepared, served, or eaten by Mayberrians, then that would be truly exciting.

And that's how *Aunt Bee's Mealtime in Mayberry* began. To bring the photographs to life even more, we've included bits of dialogue that pertain to the scenes. And, of course, the heart and soul of any cookbook are its recipes.

Instead of once again canvassing fans and members of the show's cast and crew for their favorite recipes, we decided to make this cookbook more of a thank-you gift for their support with the other two cookbooks. This time, we raided our own recipe files and those of a few family members and neighbors and came up with a collection of some of the best recipes that we have gathered through the years.

In all of our Mayberry cookbooks, we have tried to include as many as possible of the foods mentioned or seen on *The Andy Griffith Show*. We also have included other dishes for Mayberry-style foods—usually giving them Mayberryish names just to make them more fun. For this book, every recipe is inspired by a food that is actually seen or discussed in Mayberry. What we have, then, are authentic Mayberry recipes, accompanied by either a photograph showing Mayberrians with the foods or dialogue of them talking about certain foods, or both.

The other thing we have done differently for this book is that we have presented the recipes (with a couple of exceptions in order to simplify the organization) in very close to the same order that the foods appear in reruns of *The Andy Griffith Show*. So by using this cookbook you can start at the beginning of the series and essentially eat your way through the eight seasons of *The Andy Griffith Show*. That is a real challenge for any Goober. (There is a separate Table of Contents that also lists all of the recipes together by food type. This feature, along with a thorough Index, will enable you to quickly find a specific kind of recipe without having to thumb through the eight-season recipe chronology.)

Inside this book, you'll find more than 150 recipes for foods that are a part of Mayberry. A few foods from the show are not included because the references were fleeting or there weren't ideal photographs or bits of dialogue to go with them, or simply because the book could only be so big. But Mayberry fans will find most of the show's food highlights that would be expected, along with a few smaller moments with food that we hope will be pleasant surprises.

All of the recipes are different than the ones presented in either of the other two Mayberry cook-books. (Likewise, most of the dialogue and virtually all of the photographs are different than what is included in the previous two cookbooks.) There is, of course, some duplication of the types of dishes in the other books. After all, a Mayberry cookbook would be incomplete without a representation of foods such as fried chicken, apple pies, and Aunt Bee's notorious pickles.

In fact, even after all of our years of watching *The Andy Griffith Show* and working with foods related to the show, we were a little surprised by just how often folks in Mayberry eat fried chicken, potatoes, meat loaf, roasts, corn on the cob, apple pie, and a handful of other dishes. We worked to find several different and interesting variations of each of these recurrent dishes (except for corn on the cob, for which we've included just one recipe).

We've always felt that great food and Mayberry are a combination that's hard to beat. With *Aunt Bee's Mealtime in Mayberry*, we hope that you will be able to experience the feeling of enjoying both outstanding food and Mayberry in a delicious and dramatic new way.

And, finally, a Mayberry tradition that we are especially pleased to continue with this cookbook is the donation of a portion of the proceeds to the National Court Appointed Special Advocate Association (CASA). Aaron Ruben, writer/producer for *The Andy Griffith Show*, is today very involved with this organization, which works to provide advocates for children who become involved, directly or indirectly, in the nation's court system. (You can read more about CASA and Aaron Ruben's connection in a special section in the back of *Aunt Bee's Delightful Desserts*.)

Particularly given Aaron Ruben's contributions both to Mayberry and to CASA's good works, we feel that CASA is a highly appropriate organization to receive further support from a book built upon the strength of Mayberry ties.

Happy eating and reading!

—Ken Beck and Jim Clark

Aunt Bee's
Mealtime *in* Mayberry

The New Housekeeper

DICKIE THE MAGNIFICENT—*Like magic, Dickie the bird apparently can make fried chicken and biscuits disappear.*

Why the caged bird sings…When Aunt Bee first comes to live with Andy and Opie after their previous housekeeper, Rose, decides to, as Opie says, "run off and get married," Opie has trouble deciding whether he's going to like Aunt Bee. So Andy sends him to his room without dinner. But Opie's pet parakeet, Dickie, seems to have no trouble at all deciding whether he likes Aunt Bee:

ANDY: Say, Opie, you know a funny thing happened? We come back to clear the table, and you know that plate of yours and all the food on it had disappeared.

OPIE: Really?

ANDY: Yeah. And I just…(*Looks behind Opie*)…Well, I'll be dogged. There's your plate. Right there.

OPIE: Oh, yeah.

ANDY: Well, how in the world do you reckon it got all the way up here to your room—and licked clean to boot?

OPIE: I think I got a explanation, Pa.

ANDY: You do?

OPIE: Yeah, I brought it up for my bird.

ANDY: For Dickie there? Well, do you mean to tell me that he eats fried chicken and biscuits and honey?

OPIE: He loves it!

ANDY: He does?

OPIE: See how he cleaned his plate?

ANDY: You sure you ain't got a buzzard in that cage?

OPIE: *Pretty* sure.

ANDY: Dickie, if I was you, I wouldn't be doing any flying tonight because them biscuits can lay awful heavy….Say, Opie, do you reckon Dickie would like to have a nice big piece of watermelon for dessert?

OPIE: Yeah!

SAYING A MOUTHFUL—*Like Dickie the bird, Andy and Opie love watermelon as dessert following a delicious supper of fried chicken and biscuits.*

BEE LEAVING IN MAYBERRY—*Even though she has just arrived, Aunt Bee explains to Andy why she thinks it's best that she leave Andy and Opie—for Opie's sake.*

Here are two foods that Aunt Bee makes that Dickie really seems to enjoy.

Aunt Bee's Southern Fried Chicken

1 whole chicken, separated or 6 breasts
2 eggs
Salt and pepper

All-purpose flour
Canola oil

Skin, rinse, and drain the chicken. In a large bowl, beat the eggs. Roll the chicken in the eggs to coat well. In a separate bowl, mix together the salt, pepper, and flour. Roll the chicken in the flour mixture. Heat the oil in a frying pan over medium-high heat. (The oil should generously cover the bottom of the pan, about ¼ inch.) When the oil is hot, place the chicken in the pan and fry until golden brown so when you poke it the juice is clear. It will taste even better if fried in a cast-iron frying pan.
Serves 2 to 4.

Bee's Buttermilk Biscuits and Honey

½ cup butter or margarine
2 cups self-rising flour
¾ cup buttermilk

Melted butter or margarine
¼ cup honey

Preheat the oven to 425°. In a large mixing bowl, cut ½ cup butter or margarine into the flour. With a pastry blender mix until the flour resembles coarse meal. Stir in the buttermilk until the dry ingredients are moistened. Turn the dough out onto a lightly floured surface and knead lightly 3 or 4 times. Roll the dough to ¾-inch thickness. Cut with a 2-inch biscuit cutter. Place closely together on a lightly greased baking sheet. Bake for 13 to 15 minutes. Brush with melted butter.

Eating Biscuits Opie Style:
Pour ¼ cup honey and 1 to 2 tablespoons of melted butter on a plate. Using a knife, stir the butter and honey together until smooth. Dip hot biscuits into the honey mixture.
Serves about 10 people or 1 little boy and 1 hungry parakeet.

"DON'T LEAVE ME, AUNT BEE!"— *When Opie sees that Aunt Bee's getting ready to leave, he can't just stand by and let it happen. After all, he says, "If she goes, what'll happen to her? She doesn't know how to do anything—play ball, catch fish, or hunt frogs. She'll be helpless."*

OPIE: *You need me!*
AUNT BEE: *Oh, Opie, I do!*

A *happy ending to a great beginning…When Dickie flies away after Aunt Bee accidentally leaves the door to his cage open, folks wonder whether he will be gone forever. But Dickie is no dodo:*

OPIE: Pa, Pa!
ANDY: Whoa, now. Simmer down there now. You gonna bust something.
OPIE: Dickie! He's come back. Flew in the cage all by himself.
AUNT BEE: Opie, isn't that wonderful!
ANDY: Yes sir, and I told you he would, too. And I bet you that I know why. I bet you that he got out there flying around with some of those wild birds and he saw what kinda poor kinda eating they had. You know, little berries and little seeds, little pieces of roots and stuff like that, and he says to hisself, "I'm going back there to Opie where I can get me some more of that good fried chicken and biscuits and honey and stuff like that." Don't you reckon?
OPIE: I reckon.

Opie Taylor

The son of Mayberry's sheriff loves all of the things that kids everywhere do—baseball, fishing, and playing with pals like Johnny Paul and Arnold. Opie also loves to do things with his father—whether it be hanging around the courthouse, running errands, playing checkers, or just listening to his dad tell tales. Like all boys, Opie also has homework and chores to do, but he never runs low on energy, thanks to the fine meals that Aunt Bee makes sure he gets every day.

The Guitar Player

JAILHOUSE ROCKER—*Jim Lindsey is happy to sing for one of Aunt Bee's meals any day.*

Bountiful pickings:

JIM LINDSEY: You know, Andy told me you were going to have chicken and dumplings.

AUNT BEE: And that is what it is.

ANDY: Let's see, let's see. Mmm-mmm, don't that look good enough to eat!

JIM: Hey, you know something. I'd rather be arrested by you folks than anybody I know.

AUNT BEE: (*To Andy*) You coming home for dinner?

ANDY: Yes'm. I'll be there pretty soon– as soon as Barney eats. (*To Barney*) You wanna go ahead and eat?

BARNEY: Yeah, I'm about to faint.

AUNT BEE: Good. I'll have everything ready. Bye, Jim. See you next time you're dragged in.

JIM: Bye, Aunt Bee.

ANDY: I'll see you, Aunt Bee.

Jim's Favorite Chicken and Dumplings

1 whole chicken (3 to 4 pounds), cut up
Water to cover chicken
1 onion, chopped
1 carrot, chopped
Few ribs celery, chopped
2 tablespoons butter (*or to taste*)
Salt and pepper, to taste

Place the chicken in a large stewpan or saucepan. Cover with water and bring to a boil. Add the onion, carrot, and celery. Simmer slowly until tender, about 2½ to 3 hours. Remove the chicken and place in a warm covered dish. Save ½ cup of chicken broth and let cool. Season the remaining broth with butter and salt and pepper to taste. Bring to a boil and cook the dumplings.

Dumplings:
⅓ cup shortening
2 cups self-rising flour
½ cup cooled broth from chicken

In a mixing bowl, cut the shortening into the flour and stir in the cooled broth; cover and let stand about 30 minutes. Roll out, as thin as possible, on a floured board or pastry cloth. Cut into strips or small squares. Drop layers of dumplings in the boiling broth and let the broth boil over each layer before adding another layer. Cover and cook for 12 minutes. Serve hot with chicken. Dumplings may be seasoned with butter and pepper if desired.
Serves 6.

BACK IN TOWN FOR MORE OF AUNT BEE'S COOKING—*It wasn't long after Jim Lindsey landed in jail and then in Bobby Fleet's band that he was back in Mayberry and picking by the Taylor family hearth with pal Andy.*

Ellie Comes to Town

TUREENING OF THE SHREW— *Ellie Walker makes a house call on poor, ailing Emma.*

Andy and Barney pay a visit to Emma Brand, who's lying on what she believes is sure to be her death couch because new pharmacist Ellie Walker won't give Emma her special pills without a prescription:

BARNEY: Oh, hello, Emma.

ANDY: Hey, Emma.

EMMA: Sheriff...more soup?

ANDY: Aunt Bee sent it.

EMMA: Oh, how kind. Uh, just put it over there between the pork roast and the fried chicken.

ANDY: Well, it certainly is plain to see you ain't gonna starve to death.

EMMA: No, kind friends been bringing things all morning.

ANDY: Aw, ain't it wonderful how the folks help a body in a time of need.

EMMA: Bless, 'em. They want my last days to be happy ones. There's no telling how long it'll be.

When Ellie finally gives Emma her "special pills," she miraculously recovers, or was it the soup and pork roast?

Ellie's Chicken Noodle Soup

1 whole chicken (3 to 4 pounds)
2 quarts cold water
1 teaspoon salt
1 bay leaf
1 onion, sliced
2 ribs celery, chopped
½ teaspoon capers

8 ounces noodles
¼ cup butter
1 cup cream

Cut the chicken into large pieces (or just disjoint it) and place in a large pot with the other ingredients. Bring to a rapid boil and allow to simmer for 2 hours or until the chicken is tender. Remove the chicken.

Strain and chill the stock and remove the fat. Finely chop some of the meat and add it to the stock.

Cook the noodles in the chicken stock. When ready to serve add the butter and cream and reheat. *Makes 2 quarts.*

Prescription Pork Roast

1 cup dried lima beans (*soaked overnight*)
1 pork loin roast (3 to 4 pounds)
1 onion
Salt and pepper
5 medium potatoes

Drain and wash the beans. Put the roast in a crock pot with several inches of water. Slice the onion and place on top of the roast. Add salt and pepper to taste. Peel and cube the potatoes and place around the roast. Sprinkle with salt. Add the lima beans around the roast and make sure to add more water while cooking, if necessary. Cook in the Crock-Pot all day on HIGH, or for 8 hours. Remove in time for supper, or when the roast is tender. *Serves 6 to 8.*

Andy the Matchmaker

BARNEY, SAGE, MISS ROSEMARY, AND PIE—*Miss Rosemary bakes pies good enough for any fair.*

Glowing reviews:

MISS ROSEMARY: Here's that pie I promised you, Andy.
ANDY: Oh, much obliged.
MISS ROSEMARY: Congratulations, Mr. Fife.
BARNEY: For what? *(Then he glances at the newspaper in his hand that has the story about his recent heroics.)* Oh, this. Well, thanks.
ANDY: I want you to look at that blueberry pie. Ain't that pretty! Ohhh and my favorite kind, too. Miss Rosemary, you are a one for putting a glow in a man's day. I mean it. You're always so bright and cheerful.

Miss Rosemary's Simple Blueberry Pie

5 cups blueberries
1 cup sugar
1 tablespoon butter
1 tablespoon all-purpose flour
1 two-layer 9-inch pie crust

Preheat the oven to 350°. Wash the blueberries and combine in a bowl with the sugar. Dot with butter and sprinkle with flour. Place the mixture in the bottom pie shell and top with the second crust. Seal and flute the edges of the pie and poke pretty holes in the top for heat ventilation. Bake for 40 minutes. Serve with vanilla ice cream.
Serves 6 to 8.

Andy Taylor

Andy Taylor is many things to Mayberry, mainly its sheriff. But, perhaps most important, he is a father to Opie and a friend to all. The sheriff without a gun rules his town by the heart as he administers justice with a full measure of wisdom. An avid sportsman and community leader, Andy participates in plenty of well-rounded activities—from hunting and fishing to bowling and church affairs. Still, he likes nothing better than to sit back at home in the evening after a good supper, read the paper, visit with Opie and Aunt Bee, and just take it easy.

ANDY WANTS TO SEE WHAT'S THE MATTER—*"Santy Claus, did you park your reindeer out in the back?"*

Old-Fashioned Eggnog

10 fresh eggs, separated
1 cup sugar
1 cup brandy (*optional*)

1 cup rum *(Otis!)*
1½ cups cream
3 cups milk

Beat the egg yolks in a bowl until thick and lemon colored. Gradually beat in the sugar. Stir in the alcohols, if desired. Cover and chill. Immediately prior to serving, beat the egg whites and whip the cream. Stir the milk into the alcohol mixture; then fold in the egg whites and whipped cream.
Makes about 3 quarts.

Orange Dressing for Turkey

Orange you kind.

1 orange, peeled, seeded, and chopped
Zest of 1 orange
⅓ cup butter, melted
4 cups white or whole wheat bread crumbs
1 cup chopped giblets (*optional*)
½ cup chicken stock
2 eggs

½ cup dried or whole cranberries
¼ cup celery
½ teaspoon salt
Pinch ground nutmeg
2 tablespoons chopped fresh parsley
½ teaspoon black pepper

In a large bowl, mix all of the ingredients together thoroughly. (It's a good idea to add the wet ingredients a little at a time during the mixing to make sure the mixture doesn't become too wet. Moist and fluffy is ideal.) Stuff the turkey with the dressing. Seal the turkey and cook. When the turkey is done, be sure to remove all of the stuffing immediately.
Makes about 5 cups of stuffing.

PIG ON A BLANKET—*Opie just about eats his weight in hot dogs.*

Opie's fellow picnickers marvel at him:

OPIE: Why's everybody looking at me?

ANDY: Well, we got to. You got to see that to believe it. How many do you reckon have gone down that bottomless pit so far?

BARNEY: I stopped counting at four.

OPIE: *(To Aunt Bee, who's looking at the back of his head)* What ya doing?

AUNT BEE: Just checking to see if they're coming out of your head.

OPIE: Spot anything?

AUNT BEE: Not yet.

OPIE: Good, then I got room for marshmallows.

ANDY: Nooo, if you eat any more you'll swell up and your freckles will fall off.

Later…:

ANDY: You know it's a good thing that boy ain't a beaver. There wouldn't be a tree left in these woods.

A Boy's Favorite Hot Dogs

1 package of hot dogs
Several slices of packaged cheese cut lengthwise into 4 pieces (*optional*)

Preheat the broiler. Place the hot dogs in a shallow roasting pan. Put the pan on the top rack of the oven under the broiler. Cook the hot dogs for a few minutes while watching carefully. Turn a couple of times to brown all sides. They will look just like roasted hot dogs over a fire.

If you like cheese on dogs, slice the dogs lengthwise and cover with 2 pieces of cheese per hot dog. *Makes 10 hot dogs.*

Barney Fife

Mayberry's number-one deputy takes his job seriously. It's more than just a job. For Barney Fife, preserving the law is a way of life. As Andy's best friend and right-hand man, Barney makes it a point always to be armed and ready for action—with his finger on the pulse of whatever's happening in Mayberry. Though Barney's only crime is that he's attractive to women, he gives his heart to just one woman, Thelma Lou. He enjoys taking her dancing in his old salt-and-pepper suit or to the movies or maybe to the duck pond. Though his career eventually takes him to Raleigh and elsewhere, somehow, deep down, everybody knows that he'll eventually come back home to Mayberry. It's simply where he belongs.

Opie and the Bully

BOX LUNCH—*Aunt Bee prepares a piece of her delicious apple pie for Opie's school lunch.*

The Apple Pie Kid:

AUNT BEE: Remember, first you eat the sandwiches, and then you eat the apple pie. Not the apple pie and then the sandwiches. Do you understand?

OPIE: Yeah, I understand, even if it don't seem right.

AUNT BEE: Why doesn't it seem right?

OPIE: Well, if you get full before you finish, I'd sure rather leave over the pie than the sandwiches.

AUNT BEE: I know, and that's exactly why I want you to do it the other way, and don't you forget it.

OPIE: O.K., Aunt Bee. Can I have a nickel for milk?

AUNT BEE: Uh-huh. Now remember, this is for milk, not another piece of apple pie. You need that milk to make your bones hard.

And another thing:

AUNT BEE: *(To Andy)* That boy. I declare he's got the sweetest tooth I ever saw. You know if he had his way, what he'd want for lunch? Two slices of apple pie between two pieces of apple pie and a slab of apple pie for dessert.

ANDY: Now that's not surprising, Aunt Bee, considering the green thumb you've got for apple pies.

AUNT BEE: Nonsense. He's just apple pie crazy.

Apple Pie Beatrice

Crust:
1 teaspoon salt
2 cups all-purpose flour
¾ cup shortening
8 teaspoons water

In a mixing bowl, combine the salt and flour, and cut in the shortening. Add the water and mix well with the flour. Divide into four parts.
Makes 2 double or 4 single crusts.

Filling:
4 or 5 medium-size apples, peeled, cored, and thinly sliced
Ground cinnamon
¾ cup sugar
2 teaspoons all-purpose flour
¼ cup butter
Evaporated milk

Preheat the oven to 350°. Roll out 1 pie crust thin enough to fit on a 9-inch pie pan. Put apple slices in the pie shell allowing the apples to go past the rim. Sprinkle cinnamon liberally on top. In a small bowl, mix the sugar with the flour and sprinkle on top of the apples. Melt the butter and pour on top of the sugar mixture. Roll out the top crust and cut a few slits in it for steam to escape. Put on the top crust. Crimp and flute the edges. Brush the top with evaporated milk. Bake for 45 minutes to 1 hour.
Serves 6 to 8.

LADDER OF SUCCESS—*It's no sweat for Mr. Henry "Goldbrick" Wheeler to get a glass of lemonade without lifting a finger.*

Aunt Bee brings a big, tall, cold glass of lemonade for a hard-working man:

AUNT BEE: Here we are…
ANDY: *(Desperately thirsty)* Oh, man, don't that lemonade look good!
AUNT BEE: No, this is for Mr. Wheeler. He's been working on that hot roof all day.
MR. WHEELER: Dear lady… *(he drinks a satisfying swig)*. Mmm-mmm-mmm. Just hits the spot!

Lip-Smacking Lemonade

3 cups sugar
3 cups water
3 cups fresh lemon juice
16 cups cold water (or sparkling water)

In a large pot, bring the sugar and 3 cups of water to a boil and stir until the sugar is dissolved. Cover and boil (without stirring) for about 5 minutes more. Allow to cool. Add the lemon juice and the cold water and mix thoroughly. Serve over ice in nice, tall glasses.
Makes about 1½ quarts.

Aunt Bee

Aunt Bee Taylor is Mayberry's most famous cook. They didn't title her short-lived television show, shot live in Siler City, *The Mayberry Chef*, for nothing. But there was never really anything fancy about Aunt Bee's meals. She simply goes about her business in the kitchen and turns out some of the tastiest meals a body could yearn for. The superb Southern cook can whip up great casseroles, roasts, and finger-licking chicken dishes. And she can work miracles with beans and potatoes. When it comes to desserts, well, just let out the belt another notch because the incredible sweet treats that have come out of her kitchen, notably cakes, muffins, and pies, have been pleasing palates for years. Besides her cooking skills, Aunt Bee is a loving homemaker for Andy and Opie. And she loves sharing her talents in many of Mayberry's social clubs and for community events. A good neighbor to all she meets, Beatrice Taylor is definitely Mayberry's queen Bee.

The Clubmen

FINDING HIS PLACE AT THE TABLE—*In Barney's eyes, a simple meal at the Esquire Club is about to become a state dinner—Alaska that is.*

Baked Alaska

1 package chocolate cake mix

1 quart Neapolitan ice cream

Prepare the cake mix in two layer pans according to the directions on the package. You'll only need one layer (the other may be frozen for future use). Line a 1-quart bowl with aluminum foil. Pack ice cream into the bowl and freeze until firm. Cover a baking sheet with aluminum foil, and place the cake layer on the baking sheet. Invert the bowl with ice cream onto the cake. Remove the bowl and freeze the cake and ice cream until firm.

Meringue Topping:
3 egg whites
¼ teaspoon cream of tartar

6 tablespoons sugar
¼ teaspoon vanilla extract

Preheat the oven to 500°. In a medium bowl, beat the egg whites and cream of tartar until foamy. Beat in the sugar, 1 tablespoon at a time, and continue beating until stiff. Beat in the vanilla. Take the cake out of the freezer and, working quickly, completely cover the cake and ice cream with the topping. Bake for 3 to 5 minutes or until light brown. Serve immediately.
Serves 6.

The Pickle Story

LOOKING FOR A WARNING LABEL?— *Taking her life in her own hands, Clara admires a jar of Aunt Bee's pickles. (Well, after all, they do look O.K.)*

A little friendly advice for a lost cause:

AUNT BEE: What do you think, Clara?
CLARA: Oh, they're very nice, very nice indeed. They're quite pleasant and nice.
AUNT BEE: Really?
CLARA: Oh, yes. Yes, indeed. I wouldn't change them one single bit...except the brine might be just a touch too heavy.
AUNT BEE: Well, I was very careful...
CLARA: ...But that's the only thing. Maybe an extra sprig or two of parsley steeped in vinegar and possibly if you could get younger cucumbers, they wouldn't be so soft. Then drain them more and use fresher spices. But other than that, they're...quite nice...Oh, you might try boiling the vinegar just two seconds more... But they're nice.

Here are recipes for two foods that Andy incorrectly guesses are the "surprises" in the picnic basket that Aunt Bee brings to the courthouse for lunch.

Apple Crumb Pie

5 medium tart apples
1 unbaked pie crust (9 inches)
1 cup sugar
2 tablespoons all-purpose flour
½ teaspoon ground nutmeg
½ teaspoon ground cinnamon
2 tablespoons butter, melted
½ cup orange juice
Juice and rind of ½ lemon, grated

Pare the apples and grate on the coarse side of a grater; place in the pie shell. Mix the sugar, flour, nutmeg, and cinnamon in a saucepan; stir in the butter, orange juice, and the lemon juice and rind. Over medium heat, stir until the sugar is dissolved. Cool slightly and pour over the apples in the pie shell.

Topping:
½ cup sugar
¾ cup all-purpose flour
⅓ cup margarine
⅓ cup chopped pecans

Preheat the oven to 400°. In a medium bowl, combine the sugar and flour. Cut in the margarine, add the pecans, and mix until crumbly. Sprinkle over top of the apples. Bake for 5 minutes. Reduce the heat to 350° and bake for 30 minutes.
Serves 6 to 8.

Potato Pancakes

5 cups leftover mashed potatoes
1 egg, beaten
Pinch paprika
⅔ cup all-purpose flour
¼ cup butter or lard

Form the mashed potatoes into about ten equal-sized patties. Combine the egg and paprika in a bowl. Brush both sides of the patties with the egg mixture and roll lightly in the flour. Heat the butter or lard in a skillet and fry the patties in a similar matter as you would regular pancakes (cook on one side and then flip and cook on the other without fussing over and peeking at the cooking side too much before it crisps up). Serve as hot as possible. (That's one reason that these probably didn't make Aunt Bee's picnic basket delivery to the courthouse.)
Makes 10 pancakes.

KEROSENE SCENE—*"Well, that certainly is a wonderful surprise. Looka there, Barney. Aunt Bee's brought us some of her homemade pickles."*

Here are the three items Aunt Bee brings to the courthouse this fateful day:

Roast Beef Sandwiches

So far, so good.

4 slices of bread
Cold roast beef, thinly sliced
Mayonnaise
Lettuce

Generously spread the mayonnaise on one side of each slice of bread. Layer the roast beef on the bottom half (spreading additional mayonnaise between the pieces of roast beef is optional). Place lettuce on the top half adding salt, pepper, and tomato slices, if you like. Place the top half on the bottom half, pat gently, and you're done.
Serves 2.

Cole Slaw

This one's perfectly fine, too.

1 large head cabbage
1 green pepper
1 onion
1 cup sugar
1 cup cider vinegar
¾ cup vegetable oil
1 teaspoon dry mustard
1 teaspoon salt
1 teaspoon celery seed

Shred the cabbage, pepper, and onion, and mix in a large bowl. Sprinkle the sugar over the veg-etables. In a saucepan, bring the remaining ingredients to a boil; do not stir. Pour the mixture over the cabbage; do not stir. Set aside for one day or more.
Serves about 6.

Aunt Bee's Homemade Pickles

Oh, no! Say it ain't so! Surprise!

8 cloves garlic
1 onion, sliced
Peppercorns
50 medium cucumbers, washed and scrubbed clean
1½ quarts cider vinegar
2 quarts cold water
3 cups salt
4 bay leaves
16 sprigs parsley
Pinch allspice (for luck)

In the bottom of eight sterilized quart canning jars, place one garlic clove, a slice of onion, and a few peppercorns. Add as many cucumbers as will fit into the jars. In a saucepan, combine the vinegar, water, salt, bay leaves, parsley, and allspice. Let the mixture come to a rolling boil (give or take 2 seconds). Remove the parsley and bay leaves, and quickly pour the vinegar mixture over the cucumbers. Immediately seal the jars following normal canning procedures and precautions. (Wash your hands thoroughly when done.)

If you like these pickles, more power to you. If you don't, well, what did you expect?
Makes 8 quarts.

As if Aunt Bee's pickles weren't enough:

(Knock-knock, knock-knock, knock at the Taylors' back door.)
ANDY: Yo!
BARNEY: You coming to work?
ANDY: Is it 8 o'clock already?
BARNEY: Are you kidding? Three past.
ANDY: Awww. I can't hardly get started this morning. Just let me finish my coffee. Here…set down and have a piece of toast and jelly or something.
BARNEY: Yeah, I believe I will.
(Barney reaches for some toast and jelly.)
BARNEY: Nice day.
ANDY: Is it?
BARNEY: Yeah.
(Immediately after Barney takes the lid off the jelly, they both make faces, noticing a smell.)
BARNEY: You been paintin' in here?

(Barney spreads jelly on his toast.)
ANDY: No, no. Probably just some glue Opie's using on model airplanes.
BARNEY: No. Doesn't smell like glue to me. Smells more like ammonia.
ANDY: You don't reckon that gas stove's leakin'?
(Barney prepares to take a bite of toast.)
BARNEY: I found it.
(Barney hands Andy the jar of smelly marmalade and Andy retreats in disgust.)
ANDY: Aunt Bee was a-workin' in here yesterday.
(They get up and go to the cabinet and open the doors together to reveal shelves jammed with jars of marmalade.)
BARNEY: Don't tell me Aunt Bee's making marmalade now!
ANDY: Well, don't just stand there. Go get the suitcase.

Aunt Bee's Marmalade

2 pounds oranges with thin skins
Water (reserving 2 cups)

3 pounds sugar

In a large pot, boil the oranges in enough water to cover. Cook the oranges until they are good and tender. Remove the oranges from the water and dry and peel them. Reserve the peeling. Combine the sugar and 2 cups of the water in a saucepan and boil for about 10 minutes. Meanwhile, remove the seeds and pithy matter from the oranges. Add the cleaned oranges to the sugar mixture and cook for 10 minutes. Meanwhile, slice the peels into thin strips not longer than an inch. Add the peels to the mixture and continue boiling for another 10 minutes, skimming as necessary. Continue to boil until the mixture jells. Set aside for 24 hours; then pour into sterile jars and seal.
Makes about 1 dozen half pints.

Bailey's Bad Boy

THE BIG FREEZE—*Cranky Ron Bailey passes on his window of opportunity to help Mayberry folks make some homemade strawberry ice cream.*

*S*ometimes things will go bad on you when they're never around an ice cream freezer:

ANDY: Shore was good to eat, Aunt Bee.
BARNEY: Boy, was it ever.
AUNT BEE: Mmm, was good if I do say so myself. It was good. But you didn't have to stuff yourselves, you know.
ANDY: Couldn't help it. Couldn't help it.
BARNEY: (*Rubbing his tummy*) Look at that…corporation's really growing, isn't it?
AUNT BEE: Ron, did you enjoy your dinner?

RON BAILEY:	Yes, ma'am, it was fine.
AUNT BEE:	Well, I think I'll get the ice cream freezer.
ANDY:	Oh yeah, we want to make some ice cream.
AUNT BEE:	Come on, Barney, give me a hand.
RON:	You can buy it at the store. What d'you want to make it for?
ANDY:	You mean you never eat any homemade ice cream?
RON:	No.
ANDY:	You're in for a treat.

Later...:

BARNEY:	Make way for the ice cream!
AUNT BEE:	Strawberry!

Homemade Strawberry Ice Cream

½ cup sugar
¼ teaspoon salt
1 cup milk
3 eggs yolks, beaten
1 teaspoon vanilla extract
2 cups chilled whipping cream
16 ounces fresh strawberries or
1 sixteen-ounce package of frozen strawberries, thawed

Mix the sugar, salt, milk, and egg yolks in a saucepan and cook over medium heat, stirring often, until the mixture begins to bubble. Cool. Stir in the vanilla, add the cream, and stir in the strawberries. Pour into a freezer can, and you're ready to start cranking. *Makes about 1½ quarts.*

Years later, Aunt Bee still has the winning recipe:

COUSIN BRADFORD:	Strawberry, my favorite. Mmm, mmm. Oh, Bee, this is delicious.
AUNT BEE:	Thank you. I made it myself.
COUSIN BRADFORD:	Homemade, oh. I haven't had that in years.
GOOBER:	Aunt Bee makes the best.
ANDY:	First prize at the county fair.
COUSIN BRADFORD:	Really? Well, I can believe that. You know something, I've been all over the world and this is by far the best I've ever tasted.
AUNT BEE:	Well, it's just an old family recipe.
BRADFORD:	Old family recipe? Oh, my dear, these things sometimes have great value. Yes, there's a whole chain of shops selling nothing but Southern fried chicken—all based on an old family recipe.
AUNT BEE:	Really?
COUSIN BRADFORD:	Oh, yes. Ohhh, you oughta do something about this.

AUNT BEE:	Well, don't be silly. I wouldn't have the slightest idea of how to go about it.
EMMETT:	Well, you got a real expert right here in the family.

Ideas begin to churn:

COUSIN BRADFORD:	Well, it's your ice cream, Bee. It has a magic quality, a quality that could cause a major realignment in the ice cream industry. That is, if it were properly marketed.
AUNT BEE:	Oh, I knew you liked it…
COUSIN BRADFORD:	Liked it. Liked it. My dear, why, it's ambrosia. Now, my plan would be to market this ice cream, this treasured family recipe, from coast to coast.
AUNT BEE:	Coast to coast?
COUSIN BRADFORD:	That is, until we go international.
ELLA *(the gossip columnist)*:	International! Where's my pad?
AUNT BEE:	I can hardly believe my ears.

Names Cousin Bradford ponders for Aunt Bee's ice cream:

BEE'S HOMEMADE ICE CREAMS   MAYBERRY PRIDE ICE CREAMS

BRADFORD INTERNATIONAL ICE CREAMS

Guess which name Bradford favors.

HAPPENINGS IN ICE CREAM— *Everybody enjoys Aunt Bee's homemade strawberry ice cream.*

Aunt Bee's Kitchen

If there's any place in Mayberry that feels like home, it's Aunt Bee's kitchen. Better yet, it even smells like home. The kitchen is actually quite small. The table will seat only four comfortably, but Andy, Opie, and Aunt Bee generally use it just for the breakfast meal. Of course, many mornings Barney will pop in through the back door and pull his own special cup out of the cabinet (the one with the giant "B" on it), so he can enjoy a quick cup of Aunt Bee's fresh, hot coffee.

Most of the time, we see Aunt Bee's kitchen from the viewpoint of her stove, which is against a side wall. As you enter the kitchen from the backdoor (which leads into the backyard and is generally open during the spring and summer so you'll have to open the screen door), you'll notice cabinets to your left as well as the sink and a toaster on the counter. Between the toaster and the sink is a canister set decorated with flowers. There are curtains above the sink window and from here Aunt Bee can look out into the backyard. On the wall to the right of the sink is where she usually keeps her match holder.

Against the opposite wall is the refrigerator (generally loaded with leftovers) and the telephone. And against the back wall is the cabinet with the blue willow pattern dishes that the Taylor family uses for almost every meal.

This kitchen is the place where Aunt Bee works her magic. On Sundays, she whips up her great fried chicken or roast beef for dinner. And in the summertime, you can just about count on her homemade strawberry ice cream or fantastic pie for dessert.

But she has other specialties as well—ranging from rib roasts, beef casseroles, and potatoes, to muffins, cakes, and, especially, her apple pie, which is always a great favorite of the little boy in her life.

Is it any wonder that Andy has nicknamed her "Miss Fried Chicken" and "Miss Luncheon Tray" (the latter because of the terrific lunches she brings to Andy and Barney down at the courthouse in that giant wicker basket of hers)?

Other tasks that keep Aunt Bee busy in her kitchen are preserving and canning chores. And she loves to test her skills with culinary exhibits at the county fair. Friends and strangers alike feel at home in Aunt Bee's kitchen—from Barney, Gomer, and Goober to Helen, Aunt Nora, Uncle Ollie, and U.S. and Russian diplomats. Even old Walt the milkman delivers full milk bottles straight to the refrigerator.

While cookies and milk and coffee and cream are always available, it's Aunt Bee's genuine care and concern that keep family and friends feeling right at home in her all-American kitchen.

Aunt Bee the Warden

OTIS IS ABOUT TO POP—*"I came to fill my vase."*

Clara's Coconut Cake with Jelly Beans

Cake:
½ cup shortening
1½ cups sugar
2 eggs, beaten
1 cup milk
2¼ cups sifted pastry flour
4 teaspoons baking powder
¼ teaspoon salt
1 teaspoon vanilla extract

Preheat the oven to 375°. Grease two cake pans lined with paper. In a large bowl, cream the shortening until soft. Gradually add the sugar until well blended and fluffy. Add the eggs and milk and blend thoroughly. In a separate bowl, sift the flour, baking powder, and salt together, and add to the mixture. Add the vanilla and blend well. Pour the batter into the cake pans and bake for about 20 minutes. Place on racks to cool. When cooled, slice the top crust off one of the cake layers (this will be the bottom layer).

Filling:
1 cup shredded coconut
1 cup coconut milk or 1 cup milk and ½ teaspoon coconut extract
2 cups sugar
2 tablespoons cornstarch

In a saucepan, combine all of the ingredients. Cook over medium-high heat, stirring occasionally, until thickened (about 15 minutes). Allow to cool a little. Spread the cooled filling on top of the bottom layer and place the other layer on top.

Frosting:
1 cup confectioners' sugar
Hot water
¼ cup melted butter
1 cup shredded coconut
½ teaspoon coconut extract
Jelly beans

In a bowl, combine the confectioners' sugar, butter, coconut extract, and just enough hot water to make the frosting easy to spread. Once the cake has been frosted, generously sprinkle the shredded coconut on the cake and decorate with jelly beans.
Serves 10.

Clara and Aunt Bee, cake bakers and jelly bean police:

CLARA: Well, there's the coconut one. I think we ought to decorate it with jelly beans.

Later…:
CLARA: (*Slapping Andy's hand in the bowl of jelly beans*) Ah-ah-ah. That's for the cake.

Later still:
AUNT BEE: Oh, Andy, stop that! You're eating all of the black ones."
ANDY: Well, I like them, Aunt Bee.

RIOT IN CELL #1— "Barney! Barney! My cell is full of women! Help me! Help me!"

Otis Campbell

Otis Campbell is one of Mayberry's most congenial spirits. (Yes, he has been known to enjoy his share of spirits, too.) The happy fellow knows his way around and he even has his own key to the courthouse, his home away from home. Sometimes a glue-dipper at the furniture factory, Otis is married and has a Mayberry heritage that can be traced back to the Revolutionary War and one of his famous forefathers, Nathan Tibbs. In his ever-present white hat, disheveled suit, loose-fitting tie, and suspenders, Otis proves to be one of Barney's favorite targets for piping down. But the merry man can give it right back. Yeah? Yeah!

Andy and Barney in the Big City

MAYBERRY MENU MEN—*Andy and Barney get an eyeful of French class.*

Sack time:

ANDY:	Bye, Aunt Bee.
AUNT BEE:	No, wait. Almost forgot!
BARNEY:	What'd she forget?
ANDY:	Well, I bet you a quarter she forgot a brown paper sack full of sandwiches. I never been on trip in my life I didn't have to carry a brown paper sack full of sandwiches. Well, what'd you forget, Aunt Bee?
AUNT BEE:	Just a sack of sandwiches to eat on the bus.
ANDY:	Aw, a sack of sandwiches to eat on the bus. Bless her heart.

At the fancy eating place in the big city:

ANDY:	We better get us a waiter or somebody to tell us what these French words mean.
BARNEY:	All you have to do is point out something. That way you don't let on that you don't understand.
ANDY:	Oh, no, that's too chancy.
BARNEY:	Well, Andy, anything you point out's bound to be good. Besides you can learn a few new words.
ANDY:	No, I don't like to gamble like that, Barn. Besides, a little plain talk never hurt anybody.

(Andy signals to waiter.)

BARNEY:	Don't do that, Andy. You'll embarrass me. He'll think you're just a plain hick.
ANDY:	Well, Barney, there's worse things than being a plain hick—like being a hungry one.
WAITER:	*Monsieur?*
ANDY:	Hidee. Have you got a nice steak on here somewheres?
WAITER:	The steak—certainly, monsieur.
ANDY:	Good. Let me have a steak and a baked potato and green beans.
BARNEY:	*(Pointing to menu)* I'll have that.
WAITER:	*Escargots.*
BARNEY:	*(Pointing again)* And that.
WAITER:	*Cervelles du buerre noir.* Very good, monsieur. Thank you. *(Turning back to Andy.)* The steak, baked potato, green beans. *(Turning to Barney now.)* And snails and brains.
ANDY:	Well, Barn. You learned two new words, anyway.

Steak

¾ cup vegetable oil
1 garlic clove
2 tablespoons Worcestershire sauce
2 tablespoons lemon juice
¼ cup sherry
1 tablespoon sugar
1 tablespoon salt
1 teaspoon ground ginger
½ teaspoon oregano
1 tablespoon peppercorns
2 eight-ounce tenderloins

Combine all the ingredients, except the tenderloins, in a large bowl. Place the tenderloins in the bowl and cover. Marinate for about 4 hours in the refrigerator (or for up to 24 hours for more intense flavoring). Turn the meat over and stir the marinade at least once during the process. Cook the meat slowly, preferably over an open flame, and serve.
Serves 2.

Baked Potato

4 large white potatoes
¼ cup melted butter
1 tablespoon Worcestershire sauce
1 teaspoon sugar
2 tablespoons salt
Dash pepper

Preheat the oven to 400˚. Scrub the potatoes clean. Poke holes in each potato with a fork. In a large bowl, combine the butter, Worcestershire sauce, sugar, salt, and pepper. Roll the potatoes in the butter mixture, coating thoroughly. Place the potatoes on a pan and bake for 45 minutes. (About half way through, coat with some more of the butter mixture, if desired.) Serve with sour cream, butter, chives, cheese, chopped bacon, and any other desired condiments.
Serves 4.

Fancy French Green Beans

1 pound fresh green beans, French cut
3 tablespoons butter
¼ teaspoon chopped fresh thyme
1 tablespoon chopped fresh chives
1 squeeze fresh lemon juice
½ teaspoon salt
¼ teaspoon pepper
Water to cover
Slivered almonds, toasted

Place all of the ingredients except the almonds in a saucepan. Cover and cook over medium heat for 25 to 30 minutes, stirring occasionally. Drain and stir in the almonds.
Serves 4.

At a later dinner in Raleigh with Peggy McMillan:

ANDY: What's that?

PEGGY: Escargots, snails. You've had some, haven't you?

ANDY: No, I've stepped on quite a few of 'em in my time. But I never have eaten one of them.

PEGGY: Andy *(demonstrating proper snail-eating technique),* and then you dig your snail out with your fork.

ANDY: I believe I'll just let the snails go by.

GLOVE AT FIRST SIGHT—*Miss Peggy's wearing the sort of gloves one might recommend for handling a meal of snails in Raleigh.*

Following Andy's wise advice, let's skip the snails recipe here. But we can't cop out totally, so here, with apologies, is a recipe for brains similar to what Barney must have ordered.

Barney's Big City Brains

2 small calf brains
1 teaspoon salt

1 teaspoon lemon juice
½ teaspoon oregano

Wash the brains in cold water and remove the membranes. Completely cover the brains in water in a saucepan and soak for 1 hour. Drain and add enough boiling water to cover. Add the other ingredients. Simmer for 15 to 20 minutes. (An option at this point: the faint of heart may wish to dredge the brains in flour and deep fry them in oil in a saucepan over medium-high heat for about 20 minutes.) Cut into slices and serve with Big City Sauce.

Big City Sauce:
¼ cup fresh mushrooms
¼ cup butter
1 teaspoon minced fresh chives
1 tablespoon minced fresh parsley

¼ teaspoon salt
½ teaspoon Worcestershire sauce
1 teaspoon capers
3 teaspoons lemon juice

In a saucepan, sauté the mushrooms in the butter. Add the remaining ingredients and heat. Pour over the brains and become homesick for Aunt Bee's cooking back in Mayberry.
Serves 1.

Wedding Bells for Aunt Bee

GRAVY DISPOSI- TION— *A good mealtime conversa- tionalist like Fred Goss is easy to spot.*

*C*lean talk at the table:

FRED GOSS: Pass me that gravy, would you, Miss Bee? I think I'll make myself a gravy sandwich. Oh, be careful, careful! Ohhh, makes an awful spot.

ANDY: I guess you heard about the fellow who put the cleaning fluid right in with the gravy. That way when he got a spot on his tie, it took care of itself automatically.

FRED GOSS: Mixing those chemicals with food could be mighty dangerous.

ANDY: It was just a little joke about gravy.

FRED GOSS: Well, let me tell you, gravy is no joke, no siree. Takes a lot of work to get it cleaned off proper, a lotta good spotting. People just don't realize.

ANDY: Yeah, well, I mean, I didn't mean…

FRED GOSS: Wine stains almost as bad. You know who brings in a lot of clothes with wine stains? Mrs. Doug Palmer. She brings in Doug's suits and they got spots on 'em made from elderberry wine. Now I don't know if she knows it and far be it from me to gossip, but that's what it is—Doug hitting the old elderberry wine.

Later, on the front porch…:
ANDY: (*To Opie*) All I have to say is berry pie and customers come out of the wood-work. Well, I'll get two forks since you're up.
OPIE: Pretty soon you'll be making pie for Mr. Goss, won't you?
AUNT BEE: Well, I'll always make an extra one for you, Opie.

Mr. Goss Gravy

2 tablespoons meat drippings or 1 tablespoon butter
1½ cups water, divided
2 tablespoons cornstarch
⅛ teaspoon black pepper

In a saucepan, combine the meat drippings and one cup of the water. Cook over medium heat until hot. In a bowl, combine the remaining cup of water, cornstarch, and pepper and stir well. Gradually add the cornstarch mixture to the hot mixture and boil gently for 2 minutes, stirring constantly. (You may use a whisk to eliminate any lumps.) Season as desired.
Makes 1½ cups.

For sausage gravy, use milk instead of water. Use sausage drippings and ½ cup cooked, crumbled sausage. Makes about 1½ cups.

Good Gooseberry Pie

3 cups gooseberries, washed and drained
¾ cup hot water
1 teaspoon lemon juice
1½ cups sugar

6 tablespoons all-purpose flour
¼ teaspoon salt
1 2-layer 9-inch pie crust

Preheat the oven to 450°. Cook the gooseberries in the water over medium heat in a covered saucepan until tender, about 8 to 10 minutes. Drain the water and reserve it. In a large bowl, mix together the reserved water, lemon juice, sugar, flour, and salt, and stir into the gooseberries. Cook until the mixture thickens, stirring continuously. Remove from the heat and allow to cool. Pour into one pie crust and top with the second crust. Flute the edges and poke holes in the top for vents. Brush with butter, if desired. Bake at 450° for 10 minutes; then reduce heat to 350° and continue baking for about 30 minutes.
Serves 6 to 8.

Three's a Crowd

ANY WAY YOU SLICE IT—*Andy and Mary Simpson just aren't going to get much time alone. Barney, the pizza-phile, makes sure of that.*

Pepperoni Pizza

Dough:
1 package dry yeast
1 cup warm water
2-2½ cup sifted all-purpose flour
1 tablespoon sugar
1 teaspoon salt
2 tablespoons olive oil

In a large bowl, dissolve the yeast in warm water. Combine the flour, sugar, salt, and olive oil and add to the yeast mixture. Stir thoroughly until doughy. Knead on a floured surface. Place in a bowl greased with olive oil and grease the top of the dough. Let the dough sit while making the sauce.

Sauce:
2 6-ounce cans tomato paste
½ teaspoon salt
1 garlic clove, minced
¼ teaspoon sweet basil
½ teaspoon oregano
¼ teaspoon pepper

Preheat the oven to 450°. In a large bowl, mix ingredients together to make sauce. Spread the dough evenly over the bottom and sides of two cookie sheets. Spread sauce over the dough. Place toppings of your choice (sliced pepperoni, cooked sausage, sliced mushrooms, chopped green pepper, onion, or black olives, etc.) on the sauce. Top with mozzarella cheese and bake for about 20 minutes or until the cheese is bubbly.
Makes 2 pizzas.

Potato Salad for a Small Crowd

4 pounds red or gold potatoes, peeled
    and cooked
6 slices bacon, diced
½ cup sugar
3 tablespoons all-purpose flour
2 teaspoons salt
¼ teaspoon pepper
1 cup cider vinegar
1 cup water
4 green onions, sliced

Cut the potatoes into thin slices. Fry the bacon over medium heat in a large skillet until crisp; remove from the drippings. (If necessary, add more bacon fat to the skillet to make ½ cup drippings.) In a small bowl, mix the sugar, flour, salt, and pepper and stir into the bacon drippings to make a smooth paste. Add the vinegar and water; then boil 2 to 3 minutes, stirring constantly.

Combine the sauce, potatoes, and green onions in the skillet. Turn the heat off, cover with a towel (not a lid), and let stand at room temperature for 3 to 4 hours. Sprinkle with crisp bacon just before serving. This is best when served at room temperature or when reheated just before serving.
Serves 10 to 12.

Barney drops by to visit Andy and Mary after dropping off Thelma Lou at her house:

BARNEY: Oh, pizza! Looks like mozzarella, too. That's my favorite, mozzarella.

And it's a rerun again the next night:
BARNEY: Oooh, coffee. Boy, I sure am in luck. No pizza tonight, huh? Well, I'll go out and get some later. What'll it be tonight—mozzarella or pepperoni. You name it. Don't matter to me. I just like pizza.

Cousin Virgil

AN ACCIDENT WAITING TO HAPPEN—*Andy's about to find out why napkins should always go in laps.*

Aunt Bee's Pot Roast

3½- to 4-pound beef roast (shoulder is
 preferable to sirloin tip)
Vegetable oil
Salt
3 to 4 small onions
Carrots
Potatoes

Preheat the oven to 325°. Wash and
drain the roast. Heat a small amount of
oil in a Dutch oven over medium heat.
Salt the roast to taste, and brown both
sides in hot oil. Add the onions, carrots,
and potatoes with enough water to
cook. Cover with a lid or foil and cook
in the oven for about 3 hours.
Serves 6 to 8.

On the Virg of disaster:

ANDY: All right. Come on, everybody. Let's eat. Barn, you sit over there. Opie, you sit there, and Virgil, you sit here by me.

BARNEY: Here, sit down, Virg. Here we go. There we are.

AUNT BEE: (*Bringing in a roast on a platter*) Here we are.

VIRGIL: (*Reaching to help with the platter*) Aw, let me help you with that, Aunt Bee.

AUNT BEE: No-no-no, I can manage, Virgil.

VIRGIL: No, I got it.

AUNT BEE: Please.

VIRGIL: I got it.

AUNT BEE: You got it?

VIRGIL: Yeah.

ANDY: (*Urgently rising from his seat and grabbing the platter*) Let me have that, Virgil. See, I, uh, always serve the meat.

BARNEY: That's good, Virg. You wanna pass me that butter?

(Virgil reaches for the butter and knocks the roast into Andy's lap.)

VIRGIL: (*After a pause*): Hey, I'm sorry, Andy. I'm really sorry.

ANDY: (*Placing the roast back on the platter*) That's all right.

AUNT BEE: Well, let's start. Everything's on the table.

ANDY: Yep, it's all here. We just have to get it back in the plates.

BARNEY: Yeah, just a little accident, Andy.

VIRGIL: Still want the butter, Barn?

BARNEY: No-no-no, no, Virg. You just relax. You wanna pass me the butter, Aunt Bee?

(Virgil reaches for the butter.)

ANDY: Virgil!

LIKE FATHER, LIKE SON—*Andy and Opie relax after a satisfying meal of pan-fried fish.*

Fishin' lines:

ANDY: Wow, look at the size of that fish!
OPIE: He's a good one, ain't he, Pa?
ANDY: Good! I believe never in the history has anybody your size and weight landed a fish this big.
OPIE: You mean it, Pa?
ANDY: You know, if I didn't know better, I would swear that you was kin to Izaak Walton.
OPIE: Who's he?
ANDY: Oh, when it comes to fishing, he's the man that wrote the book.
OPIE: I bet he wasn't better than you. I bet nobody was better than you.
ANDY: I don't know. You remember Jonah—he caught hisself a whale.
OPIE: I thought the whale swallowed him.
ANDY: Well now, that's what I mean. When somebody catches a fish from the inside, that's *fishin'*.
OPIE: Oh Pa, you're just foolin'. Pa, I bet you're the best fisherman in the whole world.
ANDY: Well, I'll bet you something else. I'll bet you're the best fishing partner in the whole world.

Enough talk. Time's a-wasting!:
ANDY: Now, what say we go to shore and have us the best fish fry in the whole world?
OPIE: Hey, that's a great idea!
ANDY: A good idea. I'm hungry too.

Opie's Pan-Fried Fish

Olive oil	Salt
Fish fillets	Pepper
Milk	Butter, melted
Bread crumbs	

Lightly grease a skillet with olive oil. Dip the fillets in milk and roll them in a mixture of bread crumbs, salt, and pepper to taste. Drizzle butter over the fish and place in the hot skillet over medium heat. Cook for about 10 to 12 minutes total cooking time, turning once. (This may also be baked in a 500° oven for about the same amount of time.)
Makes 1 serving per fish fillet.

OPIE: Them fish sure was good to eat, huh, Pa?
ANDY: Yeah boy, mmm, mmm.

SOMETHING FISHY—*Once Opie realizes that Miss Peggy's a nice person who doesn't threaten his relationship with his father, he welcomes her as a "Blood Brother."*

Andy and Opie, Bachelors

Decision time:

ANDY: Your Aunt Bee give us a choice. What'll it be, chicken or pot roast?

OPIE: How 'bout if we just have some chocolate cookies and milk?

ANDY: No, no, Your Aunt Bee'd skin me alive if she thought I'd give you something like that for supper.

OPIE: But she ain't here.

ANDY: Nope, got to be something more substantial.

OPIE. How about a licorice whip?

ANDY: Naw. You need something that fills you up.

OPIE: We could chew tar. Johnny Paul Jason says tar's real good for the teeth.

ANDY: That's an old wives' tale.

OPIE: Johnny Paul ain't married.

ANDY: Well, it ain't gonna be chocolate cookies and milk and licorice and tar. Now, what'll it be? Chicken or pot roast?

OPIE: Pa, can I have a nickel?

ANDY: Is that for spending or deciding?

OPIE: Deciding.

ANDY: All right. There you are.

(Opie tosses the coin.)

OPIE: Pa, is heads chicken or pot roast?

ANDY: Pot roast.

OPIE: Then we're having chicken.

ANDY: Now, let's see, according to Aunt Bee's list….Wait…give me my nickel.

Coin-Toss Chicken with Curry

Red Curry Paste:
1 medium onion, chopped
1 tablespoon butter
1 tablespoon all-purpose flour

1 teaspoon curry powder
1 medium tomato, peeled and chopped
¼ cup chopped apple
1 tablespoon brown sugar

In a saucepan, sauté the onion in the butter over medium heat until golden. Remove from the heat and blend in the flour and curry powder until smooth. Stir in the remaining ingredients and return to the heat for 2 or 3 minutes, stirring all the time.

Chicken:
¼ cup olive oil
6 chicken breast halves
Red Curry Paste to taste
3 ounces sliced mushrooms

3 cups coconut milk
1 tablespoon salt
1 tablespoon sugar
1 teaspoon basil
2 fresh red chilies, cut lengthwise

In a skillet or wok, heat the oil over medium heat. Fry the chicken until golden brown. Add the red curry paste and sliced mushrooms. Stir fry for 2 or 3 minutes. Add the coconut milk, salt, sugar, sweet basil, and red chilies. Bring to a boil and cook about 10 minutes until done. Serve with steamed rice. *Serves 6.*

Pa's Potato Salad

3 cups diced potatoes
2 tablespoons vegetable oil
1 tablespoon vinegar
1½ cups shredded cabbage
½ cup ripe olives, diced
½ cup coarsely grated carrots
½ cup chopped pickles
2 tablespoons chopped pimientos
2 tablespoons chopped green pepper
⅔ cup mayonnaise
2 teaspoons grated onion
1 teaspoon prepared mustard
Pepper to taste

Cook the potatoes in boiling water until tender and drain. In a large bowl, toss together the potatoes, oil, and vinegar and refrigerate. In a separate bowl, combine the cabbage, olives, carrots, pickles, pimientos, and green pepper. Add the remaining ingredients and stir into potato mixture. *Serves 6 to 8.*

The Bazaar

KITCHEN CHAOS—*Another time the menfolk are left to themselves is when the women of Mayberry are arrested for gambling and are jailed by Warren.*

"Pure gala!"

When Andy and Opie are struggling to get by on leftovers (and whatever Andy can manage to fix), Miss Peggy comes to the rescue:

PEGGY: Supper's on!

OPIE: Golly, Pa, would you look at that table?

ANDY: (*Loud whistle*) Peggy, this is just pure gala!

OPIE: Can I make a wish and blow out the candles?

ANDY: Oh, no, no, no. These ain't wishing candles. This here's what you call gracious living.

PEGGY: Is it good?

ANDY/OPIE: (*In unison*) Mmm, mmm.

Though it's hard to say exactly what Peggy managed to put together for supper this night, one thing's for sure, of course: It wasn't more of the weenies and beans that Andy rustled up:

Weenies and Beans

¼ pound bacon, cut into pieces
½ cup chopped onion
1 pound hot dogs, sliced into thirds
1 can (29 ounces) pork and beans
1 can (20 ounces) lima beans
1 can (20 ounces) red kidney beans
¾ cup packed brown sugar
2 teaspoons vinegar
¾ cup ketchup
1 teaspoon mustard
½ teaspoon salt
Pepper to taste

Preheat the oven to 300°. Brown the bacon, onions, and sliced hot dogs in a large skillet. Mix the remaining ingredients in a large bowl. Combine everything into a large casserole and bake for 90 minutes.
Serves 8 to 10.

Convicts-at-Large

FACING THE FIRING LINE— *"Better phone him, Al."*

Counting on Floyd:

BIG MAUDE: All right, let's do it again and get it right or else!

FLOYD: Uhhh, one pound sugar, two pounds coffee, four dozen eggs, four loaves of bread, uh-ketchup, uh-fruit, and four pounds of hamburger.

BIG MAUDE: And...

FLOYD: Umm, umm...

BARNEY: And...and! Come on, Floyd!

FLOYD: If I try any funny business, you let Al have it.

BIG MAUDE: Sal, get going.

SMOKE SIGNALS— *"Hurry it up! Get that smoke outta here!"*

Hamburgers at Large

"Maude, Al, if those hamburgers are ruined, I won't be responsible."

3 pounds ground beef
1 large onion, chopped
1 green pepper, chopped
1 small jar mushrooms, chopped
2 teaspoons garlic powder
1 teaspoon black pepper
¼ cup Worcestershire sauce
¼ cup soy sauce
¼ cup steak sauce
1 teaspoon spicy mustard
2 eggs
½ cup oats or rice, uncooked

Mix all of the ingredients together in a large bowl. Make the patties about ¾- to 1-inch thick. Grill as desired. *Makes 10 to 12 patties.*

ONVICTSCAY EREHAY—*"That was their song!"*

The Bed Jacket

MAKING A WISH—*Aunt Bee got her new bed jacket, Andy got back his prized fishing rod from Mayor Stoner, and everybody gets some cake. Wishes just seem to have a way of coming true in Mayberry! Hey wait a minute! That chocolate cake's not Opie's! What is this—the twilight zone?*

Since Aunt Bee couldn't decide what color cake to make, how about a yellow one, but with chocolate icing, of course!

Yellow Cake with Chocolate Icing

3 egg yolks
1 cup sugar
¾ cup milk

½ cup vegetable oil
1¾ cups self-rising flour
1 teaspoon vanilla extract

Preheat the oven to 350°. Beat the eggs and sugar together in a medium bowl. While stirring, add the milk, oil, and flour alternately. Add the vanilla and mix thoroughly. Pour into two greased and floured cake pans (8 or 9 inches). Bake until done, approximately 30 minutes.

Chocolate Icing:
1½ cups sugar
2 tablespoons cocoa

1 tablespoon butter, melted
1 teaspoon vanilla extract
Milk

In a bowl, mix the first four ingredients. While mixing on low, add the milk slowly. Continue adding milk and mixing until a consistency suitable for spreading is achieved.
Serves 10.

Man in a Hurry

MR. TUCKER IS ABOUT TO LAUNCH INTO ORBIT—*"You people are living in another world!"*

Bee's Fried Chicken and Cream Gravy

1 chicken (about 3 pounds), cut up or
  1 package frozen chicken parts
Salt

Fat for frying (can use vegetable oil)
2 cups self-rising flour

If the chicken is frozen, allow it to thaw thoroughly. If possible, wash the chicken in cold water several hours before cooking; after washing thoroughly, sprinkle the chicken pieces with salt. Place the chicken in a covered dish and refrigerate for several hours. Heat the fat in a heavy skillet (about ¼ inch of fat). Dry the chicken thoroughly. Put the flour and two pieces of chicken at a time in a paper sack and shake vigorously. Do not put the chicken in the skillet until the fat is hot. Place the chicken in the hot fat, skin side down (do not crowd the pieces). If there is too much chicken for one skillet, use another skillet or fry two batches.

    After adding all of the chicken, cover the skillet. Turn the pieces of chicken about every 10 minutes. Keep the heat high enough to keep the chicken frying briskly. This will keep the chicken crisp and give a rich brown crust. Fry until tender, about 30 to 40 minutes, depending on the size of the pieces. Big pieces take longer. A very small chicken may be fried without covering the skillet.

Cream Gravy:

Fat
Self-rising flour
Milk

Salt, to taste
Pepper, to taste

After the chicken is fried, pour the remaining fat into a measuring cup. Return ¼ or ½ cup to the skillet and blend in an equal amount of self-rising flour; blend and stir until the mixture boils (about 1 minute). Blend in 2 cups of milk for each ¼ cup flour. Add salt and pepper to taste. Serve hot.
Serves 2 to 4.

BEE, ROAD WORTHY—"*Mr. Tucker, don't go just yet. There you are. Now, there's two chicken legs and a piece of cake and they're homemade and they're better than you'll get on the road."*—Aunt Bee

Chocolate Cake Charlotte

2 cups sugar
2 cups all-purpose flour
½ cup vegetable oil
½ cup margarine
1 cup water
4 teaspoons cocoa
2 eggs
½ cup buttermilk
1 teaspoon ground cinnamon
1 teaspoon vanilla extract

Preheat the oven to 350°. Mix the sugar and flour in a medium bowl and set aside. In a saucepan, mix the oil, margarine, water, and cocoa. Bring to a boil and pour over the sugar-flour mixture. Mix well; then add the eggs, buttermilk, cinnamon, and vanilla. Mix well and pour into a greased 9 x 13-inch pan. Bake for 30 minutes.

Chocolate Icing:
½ cup margarine
4 tablespoons cocoa
6 tablespoons milk
1 box of confectioners' sugar
½ cup nuts

Mix the first three ingredients in a saucepan and heat slowly until the margarine melts. Remove from the heat. Add the confectioners' sugar and nuts. Mix well and ice the cake while warm.
Serves 10.

Class Reunion

HIGH SCHOOL SWEETHEARTS—*Andy Taylor and Sharon DeSpain: "One of the great natural romances of all time."*

Reunion Punch

1 large can fruit cocktail, drained
2 two-liter bottles of ginger ale
1 large bottle (64 ounces) white
   grape juice

Use a gelatin mold to prepare an
ice ring for the punch. Add equal
parts ginger ale and grape juice
and one can of fruit cocktail to the
mold and freeze. Chill the ginger
ale and grape juice before mixing.
Add your ice ring.
Makes about 30 servings.

Alcohol and Old Lace

SMASHING BEVERAGE!—*Clarabelle and Jennifer
Morrison would've liked to have shared the recipe for
their elixir, but it has been declared illegal. Now, if it
were National Potato Week, well, then...*

Aunt Bee's Medicine Man

THE PROOF OF A GOOD MEAL—*When a man as well-traveled as Col. Harvey says his meal is enjoyable, he's not just blowing smoke—though he can do that, too. How? Because, he says, he has spent time learning the ways of the Indians. "The Shawnee. I lived among them. They're devils."*

COL. HARVEY: Miss Bee, I have dined in the finest restaurants in New Orleans, but I have never tasted food like that.

AUNT BEE: Oh, Colonel, how can you say that? It was only just pot luck, you know.

COL. HARVEY: Toosh, my dear lady, toosh. There is pot luck and there is pot luck. Not only the ingredients—it's the magic with which it's prepared, and you, my dear lady, have the magical touch. My compliments.

Potluck Ground Beef Casserole

1 pound lean ground beef
24 ounces pork and beans
1 teaspoon brown sugar
⅓ cup barbecue sauce
1 teaspoon onion flakes
1 can biscuits
½ cup grated cheddar cheese

Preheat the oven to 400°. Brown the ground beef in a skillet and drain off the fat. Mix the pork and beans, brown sugar, barbecue sauce, and onion flakes with the beef. Place the beef mixture in an 8 x 10-inch pan. Divide the biscuits in half, and lay them flat side down around the edges of the pan. Sprinkle cheese on top and bake for approximately 15 minutes (until the biscuits are golden brown).
Serves 6.

Floyd Lawson

Barber Floyd Lawson presides over the most popular gathering place for Mayberry's menfolk. A friendly fellow with gossip and jokes to share, Floyd is a dreamer. He yearns for a two-chair shop and plans to write a novel some day. His creative ways also reveal themselves in his songwriting, musicianship, gardening (don't forget those prize-winning pansies!), and acting. Like most of the men in town, Floyd enjoys fishing, checkers, and an easy pace of life, where nothing hits the spot better than a new flavor of pop down at Wally's.

The Darlings Are Coming

GETTING EVERY DROP— *Briscoe Darling sops up every bit of his first meal from Aunt Bee.*

*T*he Darling boys couldn't have said it better:

AUNT BEE: How'd you like the white beans, Mr. Briscoe?

BRISCOE: They was good!

AUNT BEE: Well, you didn't say anything.

ANDY: He ate four bowls.

BRISCOE: And eatin' speaks louder than words.

AUNT BEE: You told him to say that, didn't you?

ANDY: That's a very famous saying.

AUNT BEE: Oh? I stay in the house too much.

For a white beans recipe, there's only one that passes the Mayberry test: Doug's Great White Beans by Darling man Doug Dillard (originally published in Aunt Bee's Mayberry Cookbook *on page 155).*

Doug's Great White Beans

1 pound dried Navy or Great Northern beans
   (*grown on the Darling farm*)
4 strips of swine (*bacon*)
1 teaspoon salt
2 cups chopped ham of hog

Remove all of the rotten beans, rocks, dirt, and foreign types of beans. Wash each bean individually with a toothbrush until there's not a speck of dirt left on the beans. Boil the beans once in pure water for 2 minutes. Meanwhile fry the 4 strips of swine until almost crisp. Take the beans off the heat, drain, and rinse with hot water, so as not to put the beans into shock and cause the skins to come off. Put the beans back in clean, hot water on low heat. Render the grease and add the fried swine to the beans. Add 1 teaspoon of salt, or salt to taste, and the chopped ham. Cook on low heat for about 2 hours. The beans should not be overcooked as the soup will have the consistency of library paste. The broth should be fairly clear and the beans firm and not cooked to death. If you don't like white beans, try 'em. Remember, eatin' speaks louder than words. Bone Appetite.

   P.S. Goes well with Hoot Owl Pie.
Serves 6 to 8.

THE BUS BRINGETH— *Dud returns home after "fulfilling my country's needs." Only such a momentous occasion could bring the Darlings out of the hills to downtown Mayberry.*

Andy's English Valet

Barney arrives at the Taylor home just as Andy and Opie, both all dressed up, are sitting down for a gentlemanly supper prepared by Malcolm Merriweather:

BARNEY: Hey Ange, you wanna go up to the fillin' station and get a bottle of pop?

(A little embarrassed, Andy clears his throat.)

BARNEY: I'm sorry. I didn't realize you had company.

ANDY: We don't have company.

BARNEY: Well, why you all...you going to prayer meeting?

ANDY: Uh, well...

BARNEY: Prayer meeting ain't tonight, is it?

MALCOLM: *(Walking in from the kitchen)* I'm sorry. I forgot...*(He sees Barney.)*...Shall I lay one more plate for dinner, sir?

ANDY: Uh, wanna eat supper, Barn?

BARNEY: Uh, no, no. Matter of fact, I just got through work and was on my way home to change. *(He looks at what he's wearing.)* Just an old thing I hardly ever wear.

ANDY: Why don't you eat with us, Barn?

BARNEY: Uh, no, I better get on home. I ain't even picked out what I'm gonna wear tonight. *(He looks at his sweater.)* This darn ol' thing.

OPIE HAD IT RIGHT: *"I guess we're all in for some gracious living."*

Roly-Poly Pudding

Biscuit Dough:
2 cups all-purpose flour, sifted
3 teaspoons baking powder
1 teaspoon salt
¼ cup shortening
⅔ cup milk

Sift together the dry ingredients in a medium bowl; then cut in the shortening and blend with a pastry blender. Add the milk a little at a time while stirring with a fork. When the dough is of a consistency that can be readily handled, it's ready to roll.

Filling:
¼ cup softened butter, divided
3 cups cored, peeled, and finely chopped apples
¼ cup brown sugar, firmly packed
½ teaspoon ground cinnamon
½ cup granulated sugar
1 cup water
2 tablespoons fresh lemon juice
2 teaspoons lemon zest
Cream

Prepare the Biscuit Dough (canned biscuit dough or 2 cups of quick biscuit mix may be substituted) and roll onto an 8 x 12-inch pan. Spread 1 tablespoon of the butter over the dough. Cover the dough with the apples to within about 1 inch of the edge. In a medium bowl, combine the brown sugar and cinnamon and sprinkle over the apples. Roll up the pastry and apples like a jelly roll. Slice crosswise into pieces that are no more than 2 inches thick.

Preheat the oven to 425°. Boil the granulated sugar, water, lemon juice, zest, and 2 tablespoons of the butter, and pour the dissolved mixture into a shallow baking dish. Place the roll pieces in the sugar mixture. Top the slices with the remaining butter. Bake for 30 to 35 minutes. Serve hot, topped with cream.
Serves about 8.

This recipe gets its name from the bubbling and squeaking that takes place while cooking. It was much in evidence during the Depression because it is an economical dish and also an excellent way of using leftover vegetables. Malcolm Merriweather brought this to Mayberry from the Old Country.

Bubble and Squeak

4 cups cooked mashed potatoes
4 cups cooked cabbage, chopped into small pieces
Salt
Freshly ground black pepper
4 tablespoons olive oil

In a large bowl, mix the potatoes and cabbage and season to taste with salt and pepper. Heat the oil in a large frying pan and add the vegetables. Sauté over medium heat, pressing down the vegetables so that they form the shape of a flat cake. When one side is well browned, turn and cook on the other side. You can dress up the dish a little by mixing in some scallions, milk, and cheese.
Serves 4.

CONVERSE, OPINIONS—*While dinner cooks, Barney, Thelma Lou, Helen, and Andy have a chance to visit.*

*B*arney tries to play matchmaker for Andy and Helen Crump, Opie's new schoolteacher:

THELMA LOU:	I hope you all aren't starved. Dinner won't be for a little while yet.
BARNEY:	Oh, what's the hurry. We want to talk a little while anyway, don't we? Why don't we just sit down. Go on just have a seat. There we go.
HELEN:	Dinner certainly does smell wonderful, whatever it is.
THELMA LOU:	It's just leg of lamb.
ANDY:	Leg of lamb. Good, gooood! That's my favorite dish.
BARNEY:	Did you hear that, Miss Crump? That's Andy's favorite dish. Son of a gun. Ever since I can remember it's been his favorite dish. I bet you cook a mean leg of lamb yourself, don't you?
HELEN:	Goodness no. I wouldn't know where to start.
BARNEY:	(*Laughing apprehensively*) Oh, come on.
HELEN:	No, really.
BARNEY:	You mean you don't know how to cook leg of lamb, Andy's favorite dish?
HELEN:	No, as a matter of fact, I'm a terrible cook.
BARNEY:	(*More worried*) Oh, you're just saying that. You're being modest.
ANDY:	Barney, Miss Crump's so busy teaching all day, she don't have time to fool with cooking.
BARNEY:	(*Relieved*) Aw, yeah, I suppose that's true. But then someday when you settle down…I mean when you get married or something like that, why, you'll probably start to cook and you'll make a terrific leg of lamb, Andy's favorite dish.
HELEN:	Oh, I really doubt it.

BARNEY:	Well, holy cats! What will you feed your husband? I mean, if you get married or something.
HELEN:	Well, I suppose he'll just have to settle for frozen dinners.
BARNEY:	You're kidding!
ANDY:	Well, what's wrong with frozen dinners, Barn? They're good. I like 'em.
BARNEY:	No you don't. If you're gonna be home all day, well, then you'll have lots of time.
HELEN:	Ahh, but I won't be home all day. I'll still be teaching, I hope.
BARNEY:	(*Indignant*) You mean you're not going to give up your job when you get married?
HELEN:	Well, I hope not. I enjoy teaching.
ANDY:	Well, women don't do that anymore, Barn. This is the twentieth century.
BARNEY:	I know what century it is. Thelma Lou, don't you think we'd better start getting that dinner on?
THELMA LOU:	I don't think it's ready yet, Barney.
BARNEY:	Well, let's just check that. Excuse us.

(Barney and Thelma get up and head toward the kitchen.)

BARNEY:	Look, the sooner we get this over with, the better.
THELMA LOU:	Barney, why?
BARNEY:	Because I made a mistake, that's why! This dame ain't for Andy. We cross her off the list.
THELMA LOU:	But why?!
BARNEY:	Because she can't cook. She can't do anything.
THELMA LOU:	Barney!
BARNEY:	No, she's out. O-U-T, out! Now get the dinner out.
THELMA LOU:	But I don't think it's ready yet.
BARNEY:	Ready or not. Let's get it over with and get on with the next one.
BARNEY:	(*Turning back to Andy and Helen*) O.K., folks, dinner!

Thelma Lou's Leg of Lamb

½ cup brown sugar
½ cup salad oil
1 teaspoon grated lemon peel
¼ cup lemon juice

3 tablespoons vinegar
1 teaspoon salt
1 teaspoon dry mustard
4- to 5-pound rolled leg of lamb

In a saucepan, mix the brown sugar, oil, lemon peel, juice, vinegar, salt, and mustard. Heat to boiling, reduce the heat, and simmer for a few minutes. Remove from the heat and allow to cool.

Place the meat in a shallow glass casserole. Pour the marinade over the meat. Cover and refrigerate for at least 24 hours, turning the meat occasionally. Insert a meat thermometer in the center of the meat. Place the roast on the grill about 4 inches from the coals. Cover and grill for approximately 3 hours. The meat thermometer should register 175° to 180° when done.
Serves 8 to 10.

Leg of lamb has a always been a versatile menu item:

OTIS CAMPBELL: If you got an argument with a woman, stand up and fight it out.
ANDY: Well, fighting it out's what put you behind them bars, Otis.
OTIS: She threw a dish at me.
ANDY: Well, you swung a leg of lamb at her.
OTIS: But I missed her.
ANDY: Yeah, but you hit her mother.
OTIS: (*With glee*) Right in the mouth.

Aunt Bee learns that leg of lamb can be a great snack when big Jeff Pruitt is trying not to skip her meals:
JEFF: Mmm, Aunt Bee, that sure was good eatin'.
AUNT BEE: Well, thank you, Jeff. I'm glad you enjoyed it. I'm sorry we only had one leg of lamb.
JEFF: Oh, now, don't you worry about that. Sometimes I take on a little light dinner and later on really pack it on for supper.

Dogs, Dogs, Dogs

WOULD A GIRAFFE DO THIS TO ANOTHER GIRAFFE?—*Barney sits up and begs for Andy not to take away his treats.*

Andy raids Barney's bag lunch for something to feed the little dog that has "followed" Opie to the courthouse:

ANDY: Well, you've got three sandwiches in here.

BARNEY: Well, that's right: two for lunchtime and one for late in the day when I get my sinking spell.

ANDY: Well, we'll get you another one.

BARNEY: That's on salt-risen bread, you know.

ANDY: Well, we'll get one on salt-risen bread. There you are. (*He feeds the dog.*)…Now, let's see what else…There's a Mr. Cookie Bar.

BARNEY: Well, come on now. Don't give him my Mr. Cookie Bar. I'll want that for later on.

ANDY: Well, why?

BARNEY: Well, a slender, high-spirited person needs his sugar pick-me-up late in the day.

Though we can't know for sure what was in Barney's Mr. Cookie Bar, here's a cookie recipe you don't want to miss, bar none, mister!

Peanut Butter and Jelly Cookies

½ cup shortening
½ cup peanut butter
½ cup granulated sugar
½ cup brown sugar
1 egg
1¼ cups all-purpose flour
¾ teaspoon baking soda
½ teaspoon baking powder
¼ teaspoon salt
Jam or jelly

In a medium bowl, cream the shortening, peanut butter, and sugars. Beat in the egg. In a separate bowl, combine the flour, baking soda, baking powder, and salt. Gradually add the dry ingredients to the creamed mixture. Cover and chill for 1 hour.

Preheat the oven to 375°. Roll the dough into 1-inch balls, placing them 2 inches apart on a greased baking sheet. Slightly flatten the balls and bake for 10 minutes or until golden brown. Cool on wire racks. Spread jam on the bottom of half of the cookies. Top with the remaining cookies.

Makes about 4 dozen.

The Big House

BULBS OF VARIOUS DIMNESS—*Sorting Christmas lights on the courthouse roof hasn't affected Gomer's sniffer. He can still smell what's cooking in Mayberry.*

*B*arney *thinks he's on to something as he and Gomer, serving as the "blockhouse lookout," watch for criminals coming to bust their buddies out of the jail:*

GOMER: I think this finishes up all of the light bulbs.
BARNEY: Something's going on. I can just smell it.
GOMER: Oh, that's just wind blowing from the Diner. They got corned beef and cabbage on Tuesdays.

Gomer Pyle

One of Mayberry's most popular young men is filling station attendant Gomer Pyle. An excellent singer and dancer, Gomer is just downright nice. Though his own skills as a mechanic come and go, Gomer's always quick to lend a helping hand or borrow some tools from his cousin Goober. Gomer is a good friend to Andy and Barney and loves to fill in from time to time as a temporary deputy. He enjoys fishing, shooting the breeze with customers, going to the movies, and swigging a good bottle of pop. In fact, there are just a couple of things Gomer doesn't seem to like—namely haunted houses and spiders.

Diner Corned Beef and Cabbage

5 pounds corned beef brisket   2 heads cabbage, cored and sliced

Rinse the corned beef to remove the brine. Place the brisket in a large pot of cold water and cover. Bring to a boil and continue to boil for 5 minutes. Reduce the heat and let simmer for about 3 to 3½ hours. About 30 minutes before the meat is cooked, skim the fat from the pot and add the cabbage. Serve the corned beef, thinly sliced, surrounded by the cabbage on a large serving plate. Good condiments to accompany this dish include salt, pepper, paprika, butter, pickles, mustard, and horseradish.
Serves 8.

The Diner

The most popular public eatery in Mayberry is usually referred to as simply "the Diner." It's also known as both the Bluebird Diner and later the Mayberry Diner.

The Snappy Lunch on Main Street can give the Diner more than a run for its money.

You won't hear Mayberry folks talking about Snappy's pork chop sandwich. Maybe that's because they know that eating speaks louder than words or maybe they just want to keep it a secret. In any case, word has gotten around about this delicious sandwich and folks come from Siler City and Raleigh and beyond just to hear people talk about eating a pork chop sandwich.

But the Diner opens early and serves late, so it grabs a large percentage of those Mayberrians who eat out from time to time. Two of the Diner's biggest customers are Barney Fife and Goober Pyle. Not only do they know a good nutritional value for their dollar, but they each have a sweet tooth for the Diner waitresses, notably Juanita and Flora Malherbe, respectively. Howard Sprague is often a lunchtime patron as well.

Other favorite personalities at the Diner are Frank and Charlie, the cooks, and Olive, the waitress who works the breakfast/lunch shift.

The Diner offers a homey setting with its red-and-white checkered motif. Not only are the tablecloths and napkins red-and-white checkered but so are the curtains hanging over the booths by the windows. And, for those in the mood for music, there's a jukebox in the corner.

The Diner offers three square meals a day at affordable prices. They even have the prices of the most popular specials posted conveniently on the walls.

Barney will often go for a Diner breakfast, while Goober hits heavily on the Diner lunches—especially that meat loaf plate. And while Andy has the good fortune of eating Aunt Bee's great home cooking, he doesn't mind popping in late at night, maybe after a movie at the Grand with Helen, for a burger or a slice of one of the Diner's delicious pies.

Goober likes to eat at the counter, so he can swivel in the stool seats and always have a bottle of ketchup at arm's length, but Andy is partial to a booth for a bit of privacy when he escorts Helen.

Goober also knows all the tricks of getting the best service. For example, if you don't get there early for lunch, then all the best desserts will be gone. And he's strongly of the opinion that the Diner serves the best mashed potatoes in town, unless you get there late when they tend to turn lumpy.

Barney is big on the Vienna sausages, heavy on the tomato puree, and succotash, bread and butter included, at lunch. While late at night, after a hard day of keeping the law or filing reports, he tends to favor the chili-sized burgers, fries, rhubarb pie, and a chocolate malt.

Or he may just place an order through Sarah over the phone, since the Diner does deliver. And it "guarantees their food to stay hot—hours after you've eaten it," jokes Barney.

Among the other Diner specialties are the Breakfast Special, corned beef and cabbage, chicken croquettes, catfish casserole, pot roast plate, chicken à la king, roast beef, roast pork, chicken-fried steak, hamburger steak, steak sandwich, ham and lima beans, tuna sandwiches, root beer floats, waffles, and its desserts—especially the blueberry, peach, and apple pies.

As for other places to grab a bite in Mayberry, there's the aforementioned Snappy Lunch, the Junction Cafe (a favorite of the truckers and a place where waitress Juanita has worked), the Mayberry Hotel, the drugstore (the Businessman's Special of a tomato stuffed with avocado and raisins is not bad), Charlie Lee's Canton Palace, Dave's Coffee Shop, Duncan's Hot Dogs, Mom's Diner, the Palmerton Cafe, the Snack Bar, Murphy's House of the Nine Flavors, and the Weenie Burger.

Briscoe Declares for Aunt Bee

EAT!—
Hearty
eatin'…
and
how!

Andy spots Briscoe and the Darling boys coming out of a cafe in Mayberry:

ANDY: Briscoe Darling!
BRISCOE: Oh, howdy, Sheriff.
ANDY: What's going on? I got a call they's trouble down here.
BRISCOE: Not of my makin'.

ANDY: Well, what happened?
BRISCOE: Well, he refused to serve me and my boys.
ANDY: Whaddya do—cause trouble?
BRISCOE: Just takin' normal safeguards for eatin' in a strange place. The boys here will back me up. Ain't that right, boys?

(The boys are silent.)

ANDY: There's a lot in what they say. But I'd still like to know what you did.

BRISCOE: Well, I wanted to sit in the kitchen and watch 'em cook my meal.

ANDY: Didn't you see the sign over the door that says "help only"?

BRISCOE: Well, that's what I was trying to do. Now, it looks like me and the boys are going to have to go without supper.

ANDY: Well, maybe we can do something about that. You can come over to the house and have supper with me.

BRISCOE: Will that aunt of yourn let me set in the kitchen and watch her cook?

ANDY: She'd be honored.

BRISCOE: You know something, Sheriff? That haircut of yours may be city style, but your heart was shaped in a bowl.

Later...back at the Taylor house:

ANDY: Well, Mr. Darling, how was it? Everything to your satisfaction?

BRISCOE: Oh, that's the cleanest cookin' woman as I ever did see.

ANDY: Aunt Bee believes cleanliness is next to godliness.

BRISCOE: Neat and reverent. That's a combination that's hard to come by.

Bread!

Good
Cake like
texture

½ cup butter
½ cup sugar
3 eggs
1 cup milk
2 cups all-purpose flour
2 teaspoons baking powder
½ teaspoon salt

Preheat the oven to 350°. In a large bowl, cream together the butter and sugar. Add the eggs and beat well. Add the milk and stir well. Sift the flour, baking powder, and salt together, and add to the mixture. Stir until well blended. Pour the batter into a greased 9 x 12-inch pan and bake for about 30 minutes. Cut into rectangles and serve with butter. *Makes 12 hearty-eatin'-sized pieces.*

Taters!

See the recipe on page 160.

Meat!

1 3- to 4-pound beef brisket or beef roast
6 small onions, chopped
8 medium carrots, chopped
5 potatoes, peeled and quartered
1 medium green cabbage, cut into wedges

Put the beef into a large pot and cover with cold water. Cover and simmer for 3 to 4 hours or until tender. Skim the fat from the liquid and add the first 3 vegetables. Cover and simmer for 20 minutes. Remove the meat and keep warm. Add the cabbage to the broth and simmer uncovered for 10 to 15 minutes until all of the vegetables are tender. *Serves 6 to 8.*

Pearly Onions

2 cans (10 ounces each) pearl onions
3 tablespoons margarine
3 tablespoons all-purpose flour
½ teaspoon salt
¼ teaspoon pepper
2¼ cups milk
2 packages (10 ounces each) frozen peas, thawed

In a pot, cook the onions in boiling water. Reduce the heat to low, cover, and simmer until tender. Drain and cool. Peel the onions, leaving a little at the root end so the onions will hold their shape. Next, melt the margarine in a saucepan. Stir in the flour, salt, and pepper. Gradually add the milk, stirring constantly until the sauce thickens. Combine the onions and peas in a skillet and pour the sauce over the vegetables. While continuously stirring, cook until heated through. *Serves 6.*

The Darlings

Briscoe Darling, his daughter Charlene, and four sons are Andy's favorite family from the mountains around Mayberry. The music-making folks from the other side of the Robert E. Lee Natural Bridge enjoy their visits to Mayberry, too—especially when they get to have helpings of some of Aunt Bee's delicious cooking. When they've had their fill of city life, they just hop back on the truck and head home to their cabin in the hills on that land of theirs that's blessed with good strong boulders.

Everybody gathers at the table:

ANDY: Oh, Aunt Bee those potatoes are a picture no artist could paint.

AUNT BEE: Oh, flibbertigibbet!

ANDY: (*Laughing*) She can't stand to be bragged on.

BRISCOE: Fine quality. I like modesty in a human female being.

ANDY: Yeah. Ope, pass the bread to the boys.

OPIE: O.K., Pa.

(The bread plate makes its way around the table and arrives empty at Briscoe.)

BRISCOE: BREAD!

AUNT BEE: (*Rushing in from the kitchen*) What happened?!

ANDY: Mr. Darling put in a request for additional bread, Aunt Bee.

BRISCOE: Oh, didn't I yell loud enough?

AUNT BEE: Oh, you must be big eaters.

BRISCOE: Oh, we're knowed as a family of hearty eatin' men and beautiful, delicate women.

ANDY: Hmm. Here, help yourself to the potatoes, boys. Good.

(The plate of potatoes makes its way around the table and arrives empty at Briscoe.)

BRISCOE: TATERS!

ANDY: How about when you want something, just tell me and I'll tell Aunt Bee.

BRISCOE: Oh, that's a good idea.

(Looking a bit frazzled, Aunt Bee enters the room.)

ANDY: Aunt Bee, we need some more potatoes.

BRISCOE: Sure does look good, don't it.

ANDY: It does.

OPIE: MEAT!

ANDY: Ope! Aunt Bee will see what we need when she comes in.

ANDY: (*To Briscoe*) I don't like for the boy to raise his voice at the table.

BRISCOE: Oh, you gotta watch that. Hear that, boys? No yellin' at the table. It'll take a while, but I'll learn 'em.

(Aunt Bee returns with more meat and takes her seat at the table.)

BRISCOE: Did you get some meat?

ANDY: Oh, yeah, we got meat.

BRISCOE: Something restin' uneasy on your mind, ma'am?

AUNT BEE: No-no. I was just admiring your hearty appetite.

BRISCOE: I bet it does your heart good to see a real eater at work, huh?

AUNT BEE: Well, Andy and Opie are pretty good eaters. Oh, here, you don't have any butter on your baked potato.

BRISCOE: Thank you, ma'am, for your kind attention.

ANDY: You all cookin' for yourselves now that Charlene's married, are you?

BRISCOE: Oh, the boys there, they been takin' turns. They're just about the worst cooks they is. Just the other night, they cooked up about the worst mess of grub I ever did see.

ANDY: Oh?

BRISCOE: Hoot owl pie. Perfectly good hoot owl— just plum wasted.

ANDY: That's a shame.

AUNT BEE: Oh, you poor man. Here, have some more of my pot roast.

BRISCOE: Thank you, ma'am.

AUNT BEE: Now, do you like the pearly onions?

BRISCOE: Oh, they twang my buds.

AUNT BEE: Well, you don't have any. There you are.

BRISCOE: Thank you. You know, it appears to me like you're specializing on me. What about the sheriff and the boy here? They ain't eat enough to keep a June bug alive.

AUNT BEE: Well, they have meals like this every day. You're a special guest, Mr. Darling.

ANDY: That's right, Mr. Darling. Don't worry about us. You just dig in there and enjoy yourself.

OH, MEN OF THE OWL—*This owl had better keep an eye out for the Darlings if it doesn't want to wind up in a pie.*

Mountain Pie

½ cup butter
1 cup sugar
1 cup self-rising flour
¾ to 1 cup milk
4 cups fruit of choice

Preheat the oven to 350°. Melt the butter in a baking dish. In a medium bowl, combine the sugar and flour. Stir in the milk. Pour mixture into the butter in the baking dish. Mound the fruit into the dish. Bake for 30 to 45 minutes or until browned.
Serves 6.

*A*ll done?:

AUNT BEE: More pie,
Mr. Darling?
BRISCOE: I'm ample ma'am.
Three cuts of pie is
my high-water
mark.

It's no wonder that Briscoe was full. Aunt Bee also served tomatoes and even some pickles as part of this hearty meal.

Gomer the House Guest

PUTTING HIS BEST FEET FORWARD—*Gomer enjoys a TV dinner with the Taylors.*

When Wally fires Gomer for being "insufficient" in his duties, Gomer loses his place to stay (including his kitchenette) in back of the fillin' station:

GOMER: I come to see you. I was wondering if you could put me up in a cell till I settle on my feet someplace.
ANDY: I'll go you one better than that, Gomer. Come over to the house and stay with me and Opie and Aunt Bee for a few days.
GOMER: Oh, that's putting you out.
ANDY: Glad to have you. We got more room than we know what to do with.
GOMER: Well, it don't seem right.
ANDY: You oughta see the fried chicken Aunt Bee's got to throw out.
GOMER: I accept.

Home Fried Chicken

2 eggs
2 chickens (2 to 3 pounds of chicken)
2 cups all-purpose flour

Salt and pepper to taste
Paprika to taste
2 cups lard

In a small bowl, beat the eggs and coat the chicken with the egg batter; then mix together in a large bowl the flour, salt, pepper, and paprika, and roll the chicken in the mixture. For the best fried chicken, fry in pure lard in a large skillet over medium-high heat. Once the lard is hot, add the chicken. Cover and cook for about 25 minutes; then keep turning it so as to brown on all sides. Then cook uncovered for about 20 minutes.

If you choose to use cooking oil instead of lard, then add 2 tablespoons of butter to help the chicken brown.
Serves 4.

Ernest T. Bass Joins the Army

WHEN YOUR WHOLE BODY'S A WEAPON, IT NEEDS AMMUNI-TION—*Not to mention that Mr. Cookie Bar late in the afternoon.*

*B*arney the quartermaster:

OLIVE: Good morning, Barney.

BARNEY: Hi, Olive. Nice day, huh?

OLIVE: Say, you and Andy left an extra quarter yesterday. I'm sure it was a mistake.

BARNEY: What do you mean mistake? That was your tip!

OLIVE: Two quarters? But you never…

BARNEY: Olive! What do you think you're dealing with? A couple of pikers? You got yourself a half a C tip. Enjoy it!

BARNEY: Let's see. I'm not too hungry this morning. I'll have uh...orange juice, bowl of cereal, stack of wheats, three eggs over (make sure they ain't runny now, Olive), bacon on the crisp side, white toast, buttered, hash brown potatoes, and coffee—coffee and cream.

OLIVE: Does my heart good to see a thin person eat.

Stack of Wheats

½ cup whole wheat flour
¾ cup self-rising flour
½ teaspoon baking soda
2 tablespoons sugar
1 egg
1 cup buttermilk
3 tablespoons melted shortening

In a large bowl, sift together both flours, the soda, and sugar. Beat the egg in a separate bowl and add the buttermilk and shortening. Add the liquid ingredients to the dry ingredients and stir just until blended. The batter should be a bit lumpy. Heat the skillet or griddle until a drop of water will dance about on it. (If it goes up in steam immediately, then the surface is too hot.) Pour the batter, ¼ cup for each wheatcake, on the hot skillet. Cook on one side until the cake is full of bubbles that have not popped. Turn and cook on the other side. Serve hot. If the batter gets too thick, thin with a little water.
Makes 1 Barney-sized stack (about 8 wheats).

Ernest T. Bass

Ernest T. Bass doesn't chew his cabbage twice. In fact he doesn't chew anything twice, but the renowned rock thrower does wash his food before he eats it, and he breathes through his nose to help him talk whilst he eats. The zany character from the mountains specializes in breaking windows but quite often ends up with his own broken heart because of his failed chances at romance—notably with Charlene Darling and Hogette Winslow. But, with Andy and Barney's aid, Ernest T. attends Mrs. Wiley's society party and meets the girl of his dreams, the sweet "Romeena." That's an encounter that makes him a happy nut.

Hash Brown Potatoes

½ cup margarine, melted
8 ounces sour cream
1 can (10¾ ounces) cream of chicken soup
1 package (2 pounds) frozen hash browns
  (*Southern style*), thawed

½ teaspoon salt
¼ teaspoon pepper
½ cup chopped onion
2 cups grated Cheddar cheese
Vegetable oil

Preheat the oven to 350°. In a large bowl, mix the margarine, sour cream, and soup together. Put the hash browns in a separate bowl. Add the salt, pepper, and onion. Pour in the soup mixture and stir well. Mix in the cheese. Coat a 9 x 13-inch dish with vegetable oil. Pour the mixture in the casserole. Bake for 45 minutes. *Serves 6.*

The Banjo-Playing Deputy

MAN OF THE CLOTH— *Visitor Jerry Miller fumbles his exit from the dinner table.*

The Sermon for Today

AMEN TO THIS—"Slow down. Take it easy. What's your hurry? What indeed, friends, is your hurry?"

*A*ndy and Barney sitting on the front porch after Sunday dinner:

BARNEY: Yeah, we really packed her away, didn't we?

ANDY: Yeah, boy.

BARNEY: (*Pats tummy*) Fortunately, none of mine goes to fat. All goes to muscle.

ANDY: Does, huh?

BARNEY: That's a mark of us Fifes. Everything we eat goes to muscle. (*Pats his tummy*) See there?

ANDY: I see.

BARNEY: My mother was the same way. She could just eat and eat and eat…

ANDY: Never went to fat, huh?

BARNEY: (*Nods*) Know where it went?

ANDY: Muscle?

BARNEY: Yeah. That was a mark of us Fifes…

ANDY: Good…you know what I believe I'll do? Run down to the drugstore and get some ice cream for later.

BARNEY: You want me to go? I'll go.

ANDY: No, I'll go.

BARNEY: Well, I don't mind going.

ANDY: I don't either. I'll go.

BARNEY: You're probably tired…. Why don't you let me go?

ANDY: No, I'm not tired. I'll go.

BARNEY: Well, I sure don't mind going.

ANDY: You sure?

BARNEY: Uh-huh.

ANDY: Why don't we both just go?

BARNEY: O.K.

ANDY: You ready?

BARNEY: Uh-huh.

ANDY: Well, let's go.

BARNEY: Where we goin'?

ANDY: Down to the drugstore to get some ice cream for later.

BARNEY: O.K.

ANDY: Come on.

(*Both slowly rise as Aunt Bee comes out on the porch.*)

AUNT BEE: Andy, where you boys going?

ANDY: We thought we'd run down to the drugstore and get some ice cream for later.

AUNT BEE: Well, why do you want to *run* to the drugstore, as if it couldn't wait…

ANDY: Ma'am?

AUNT BEE: Well, that's just what the preacher was talking about this morning. It seems as if nothing can wait. Everything is rush, rush, rush!

(*Andy and Barney slowly sit back down.*)

Opie's Ill-Gotten Gain

THE "B" STANDS FOR BARNEY—*Barney enjoys coffee in his special mug when he stops by to pick Andy up for work.*

Meanwhile, Opie's getting ready to leave for school:

AUNT BEE: Did you get your nutrition money?
OPIE: Yep, got it in my shoe.
BARNEY: Nutrition money?
AUNT BEE: Uh-huh, They get a mid-morning snack. Helps their concentration. Opie! Opie! Your lunch!

That nutrition money must have really paid off!:
ANDY: Did you hear that, Aunt Bee? What do you think of a boy who gets all A's?
AUNT BEE: I know. Isn't it wonderful?
OPIE: I fooled you, didn't I? You thought there were going to be some bad marks there, but I fooled you, didn't I?"
ANDY: You sure did, you little buzzard. Am I ever proud of you. Aunt Bee, what are we gonna do to reward a boy like this?
AUNT BEE: I baked him a special pie.
ANDY: You did?
AUNT BEE: Um-huh, his favorite—butterscotch pecan.
ANDY: Mmm, mmm.
OPIE: A whole pie just for me?
ANDY: Why not.
AUNT BEE: Well, your head's so full, we might as well fill your tummy to balance you.
ANDY: That's right. Fill up your tummy. Anybody who gets all A's ought to have a little tum-tum full of pie-pie-pie.

Opie's Butterscotch Pecan Pie

½ cup margarine, melted
4 eggs, beaten
1 cup sugar
1 cup light corn syrup

2 eight-inch pie crusts
1 cup pecans, chopped
1 package (6 ounces) butterscotch morsels

Preheat the oven to 350°. In a large bowl, beat together the margarine, eggs, sugar, and syrup. Pour equal amounts into both pie shells. Top both pies with equal amounts of the nuts and morsels. Bake for 50 minutes. *Makes 2 pies.*

Up in Barney's Room

QUICK!—*Hide the chili before Mrs. Mendelbright finds it!*

*A*ndy drops by Barney's room at Mrs. Mendel-bright's Boarding House:

BARNEY: I thought you was Mrs. Mendelbright.
ANDY: Oh, cookin' supper, huh?
BARNEY: Yeah.
ANDY: Oh, chili.
BARNEY: Yeah, I make it myself.
ANDY: Boy, got a lot of spices in there.
BARNEY: Well, it's just loaded with herbs.
ANDY: Just smelling it makes my head all wet.
BARNEY: You wanna stay for supper?
ANDY: Uh, no thanks.
BARNEY: Well, I got plenty.
ANDY: No, no. I'll go on home.
BARNEY: You sure? A little chili? A little sweet cider?
ANDY: Oh, no thanks. Oh, here's your pay-check. Sorry I couldn't get over here in time for you to make the bank. You could've eaten out for supper.
BARNEY: Oh, that's all right. I get so sick of eating out. You sure you won't have some of that?
ANDY: Oh, no thanks.
BARNEY: Here. Just taste it.
ANDY: No-no.
BARNEY: Taste that.
ANDY: No thanks.
BARNEY: You're missing out on a good thing.

Barney's Chili

1 pound lean ground beef
1 garlic clove, minced
1 onion, finely chopped
1 green bell pepper, finely chopped

1 package chili seasonings
1 can (8 ounces) tomatoes, finely chopped
1 can (16 ounces) kidney beans
1 cup grated Cheddar cheese

Brown the beef, garlic, onion, and green pepper in a large pan over medium heat. Add all the remaining ingredients, except the cheese. Cook at a robust simmer for 1 hour. Just before serving, add the cheese. *Serves 6.*

Later, after the chili has been left cooking unattended for a while:

ANDY: Chili's burning! How you turn this thing off?!
BARNEY: Pull the plug.
ANDY: You reckon Mrs. Mendelbright smelled it?
(Knock-knock-knock at the door.)
ANDY: She smelled it!

TOO LATE!— *She smelled it! Pack your bags, Barney.*

Opie and His Merry Men

RICH EXPERIENCE—*Opie and his pals learn firsthand about the world of Robin Hood.*

Time for a feast:

HOBO: Say, fellas, I wish I could invite you to have some lunch with me, but all I got here is some Mulligan stew and not too much of that.

OPIE: We brought our own lunch.

JOHNNY PAUL: Yeah, we're cooking it back in the woods.

HOBO: Really? What you got?

OPIE: Well, it's just weenies.

JOHNNY PAUL: And root beer.

HOBO: Weenies and root beer. Is that so? Say, I got an idea. Why don't you boys bring your stuff over here and we'll have ourselves a barbecue—Robin Hood style?

OPIE: Whatd'ya say?

BOYS: Yeah!

Mulligan Stew

1 pound stewing beef, cubed
1 stewing chicken, cut into large pieces
3 quarts chicken stock or water
2½ cups tomatoes, quartered
1 can (16 ounces) kidney beans
1 cup chopped carrots
1 cup chopped celery
1 cup chopped onions
2 cups diced potatoes
2 tablespoons Worcestershire sauce
1 bay leaf
Salt and pepper, to taste

In a large stew pot, bring the first 3 ingredients to a boil and simmer for 1½ hours. Cool a little and remove the chicken bones. Add the remaining ingredients and simmer for about 1½ hours more, stirring often. This should be enough for Robin Hood and all of his Merry Men (and it freezes well, too), but if there's not enough stew to go around, supplement it with weenies and root beer.
Makes 6 to 8 servings.

Hobo Weenies and Root Beer

½ cup ketchup
¼ cup butter
1 garlic clove, minced or ¼ teaspoon
    garlic powder
1 teaspoon Worcestershire sauce
¼ cup brown sugar
Water (if necessary to thin)
1 package hot dogs

In a medium bowl, stir the first five ingredients together and add enough water so that it is not too thick. Cut each hot dog into thirds. In a crock pot combine the hot dogs with the barbecue sauce. Cook on LOW all day and serve with your favorite brand of root beer.
Serves 4 to 5.

---

*D*inner table wisdom:

BARNEY: You see, Ope, it ain't only the materialistic things in this world that makes a person rich. There's love and friendship—that can make a person rich.
AUNT BEE: Very nicely put, Barney.
ANDY: I don't believe I ever heard that said any better.

BARNEY: Yes sir, Ope, it ain't only the materialistic things in this world that makes a person rich. You know what else does? Love and friendship.
ANDY: That's right.
BARNEY: I bet you thought it was only the materialistic things, huh? Well, it ain't.
ANDY: There's love and friendship.

HAPPINESS IS—*Enjoying a good square meal of meat loaf with family and friends.*

Didn't anybody plan ahead and save room for dessert?:

AUNT BEE: Well, I just took an apple pie out of the oven. Who's for apple pie?
OPIE: I don't care for any.
AUNT BEE: No pie?
ANDY: Well, I'll have to confess I can't take any either.
AUNT BEE: Oh, Andy.
ANDY: No, ma'am. Just one more little bite of meat loaf here and that'll kind of fill in the chinks.
AUNT BEE: Barney, you won't let me down.
BARNEY: Oh, no thanks. I'm kind of watching the old carbohydrates and glucose this week. Apple pie is just loaded with carbohydrates and glucose.
AUNT BEE: Well, heaven knows I shouldn't eat any.
BARNEY: Not if you're watching the old carbohydrates and glucose, you don't.

A new twist for Aunt Bee:

ANDY: Mmm, mmm!
AUNT BEE: I never thought I'd change my apple pie recipe, but Clara said she put a pinch of nutmeg in the apples while they're simmering, and I thought I'd try it.
ANDY: I think it picks it up.
AUNT BEE: Mmm, thank you.

Aunt Bee's Meat Loaf

1½ pounds ground beef
1½ cups rolled oats
1 medium onion, chopped
1¼ teaspoons salt
¼ teaspoon black pepper
2 tablespoons vinegar

2 tablespoons prepared mustard
1 egg
2 tablespoons brown sugar
1½ cups milk
15 ounces tomato sauce

Preheat the oven to 350˚. In a large bowl, mix together all of the ingredients except the tomato sauce, and shape into a loaf. Place in a Pyrex dish. Pour the tomato sauce over top. Cook for about 1 hour.
Serves 4 to 6.

Aunt Bee's Missing Apple Pie

8 Granny Smith apples
¼ teaspoon ground nutmeg
1 cup sugar
3 tablespoons all-purpose flour

Dash salt
1 teaspoon ground cinnamon
Two-layer 9-inch pie crust
¼ cup butter, softened

Preheat the oven to 400˚. Peel and thinly slice the apples. Toss the apples in a bowl with all of the dry ingredients. Place the bottom crust in a 9-inch pie pan and dot with half of the butter. Place the apples in the pie crust in the pan and spread evenly. Dot the apples with the remaining butter. Cover with the second pie crust, flute the edges of the pastries to seal, and cut attractive vents in the top for releasing the heat. Bake for 45 to 60 minutes or until golden brown.
Serves 6 to 8.

Barney and the Cave Rescue

A REAL STRAIN—*"Boy, you sure couldn't ask for a better day for a picnic. Yes sir, Helen's made an apple crumb pie. That on top of Thelma Lou's fried chicken. Hey, boy, we'll be in for a strain on the old suspender buttons."*—Andy Taylor

Thelma Lou's Semi-Fried Chicken

3 pounds fryer parts
All-purpose flour
½ cup shortening
2 teaspoons salt

Dash pepper
2 tablespoons all-purpose flour
2 cups whole milk

Preheat the oven to 350°. Rinse the chicken pieces in water and roll them in the flour. Heat the shortening in a large skillet. Quickly brown the chicken on all sides. Cover and cook until tender. Add the salt and pepper during the last 20 minutes. Remove the chicken from the skillet. Add the 2 tablespoons of flour to the fat in the skillet. Brown the chicken in the mixture. Add the milk and cook the chicken for 5 minutes more. *Serves 4.*

See Aunt Bee's recipe for Apple Crumb Pie (which Aunt Bee likely shared with Helen) on page 39.

Thelma Lou

Thelma Lou and Barney have great times together. One of the few things ever to come between them is a pan of cashew fudge. They especially enjoy double-dating with Andy and Helen. Thelma Lou's a patient lady, who puts up with all kinds of nutty antics by her true love. But nobody understands Barney better than Thelma Lou. What she understands most of all is that he's quite a guy. Someday they'll be together forever and everyone will know that her last name is Fife. It's just one of those things that's meant to be.

NOT NO 'COUNT—*One potato, two potato, three potato, four…*

Flingable Bread

1 package active dry yeast
2 cups warm water
1 tablespoon salt
2 teaspoons sugar
1 tablespoon softened butter
5½ cups all-purpose flour, divided
Cornmeal

In a large bowl, stir the yeast into the warm water until dissolved. Add the salt, sugar, butter, and 2 cups of the flour; with a wooden spoon, beat until smooth, about 2 minutes. Gradually add the remaining flour, mixing in the last of it by hand until the dough leaves the side of the bowl. Turn the dough onto a lightly floured board. Knead until it is smooth and elastic, about 10 minutes. Place the dough in a lightly greased bowl; turn the dough over to grease both sides. Cover with a towel; let it rise in a warm place (85°), free from drafts, until it doubles in bulk, about 90 minutes.

Preheat the oven to 400°. Lightly grease a large cookie sheet. Sprinkle with cornmeal. Punch down the dough and turn onto a floured board. Divide the dough in half. With the palms of your hand, roll each into a 36-inch-long rope. Twist the dough into 2 spiral loaves, each about 10 inches long. Place on the prepared cookie sheet. Brush with cold water. Let the dough rise, uncovered, in a warm place, free from drafts, until it doubles in bulk (about 90 minutes). Brush the top with water. Place a shallow pan of water on the oven bottom. Bake the loaves for 30 to 45 minutes, brushing with water every 15 minutes. Remove the loaves to a wire rack for cooling.
Makes 2 loaves.

Baked Potato

See the recipe on page 51.

Bargain Day

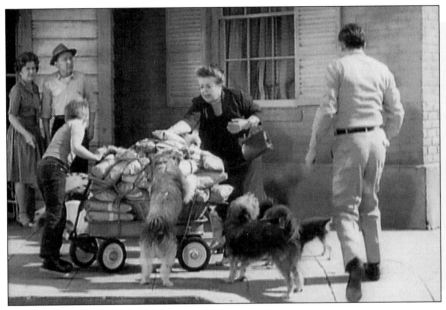

Things are getting pretty hot:

ANDY: Aunt Bee, what's going on? What's in there?

AUNT BEE: The beef, Andy. Will you get the dogs away?

ANDY: The meat? Where you taking it?

AUNT BEE: To Mr. Foley. He offered to store it for me. Would you do something!

ANDY: Aunt Bee, I ain't going to let you do it.

AUNT BEE: What?!

ANDY: I'm not going to have Mr. Foley putting himself out for our mistake. Now you better get that meat back home…

AUNT BEE: But Mr. Foley said that…

ANDY:	I don't care what Mr. Foley said. It's not fair. Now it's our problem and we'll solve it.
AUNT BEE:	Well, how, for heaven's sakes?!
ANDY:	We'll call the man from Mt. Pilot to come over to fix the freezer. He'll come first thing in the morning. It's what we should have done to start with.
AUNT BEE:	Well, the meat will defrost!
ANDY:	Not if you get it back in the freezer and keep the lid closed!
AUNT BEE:	But Mr. Foley…
ANDY:	Get the meat back in the freezer!
AUNT BEE:	But…
ANDY:	Call the man!
AUNT BEE:	Come on, Opie.

(Aunt Bee and Opie head back home, but she pauses.)

ANDY:	Call the man!

Bargain Beef Brisket

4 pounds beef brisket
2 onions, sliced
2 carrots, sliced
2 ribs celery, chopped
Salt and pepper to taste

Place the brisket in a deep pot and add enough water to completely cover the meat. Bring to a slow boil; then simmer for 3 hours. Add the remaining ingredients and simmer for 1 hour more. Remove the brisket to a serving plate. Thicken the remaining liquid for gravy and serve on the side.
Serves 8.

It's tough to surprise Andy:

OPIE:	Hi, Pa! Surprise!
ANDY:	Oh, what's the surprise?
OPIE:	I can't tell you. Aunt Bee said not to.
ANDY:	Boy, something smells good.
OPIE:	You're not supposed to notice.
AUNT BEE:	Andy, you're late.
ANDY:	I'm sorry, Aunt Bee. Things came up.
AUNT BEE:	Well, supper's all ready. Now, Opie, seat your father.
ANDY:	Candles? What's going on?
AUNT BEE:	Well, I don't see why we can't have candles.
OPIE:	Sit down, Pa.
ANDY:	No tricks, now.
OPIE:	I won't.
ANDY:	O.K. It looks like a party. Roast beef and no company?!
OPIE:	Are you surprised, Pa?
ANDY:	Well, I sure am. What is it, somebody's birthday?
AUNT BEE:	Well, I thought we oughta have a decent supper for once.
ANDY:	Well, boy, folks are really gonna say we're getting uppity. Having roast beef and it ain't even the weekend.
OPIE:	Is it O.K. if I start?
AUNT BEE:	No, wait until your father has his.
ANDY:	Well, my goodness. We are formal this evening. On your mark, get set, go!

The Return of Malcolm Merriweather

Barney, pacing in the courthouse, is becoming alarmed that his lunch hasn't arrived yet:

ANDY: Will you settle down? You're gonna wear a groove in the floor.

BARNEY: Well, where's Aunt Bee with lunch? She's usually here and gone by now.

ANDY: She's a little late.

BARNEY: Well, I'm hungry, Ange.

ANDY: She'll be along in a few minutes. Relax.

BARNEY: I happen to have this low sugar-blood content, and if I don't get my lunch by noon, then I get a headache and I'm no good to anybody.

ANDY: A few minutes one way or the other shouldn't make any difference.

BARNEY: Well, it does to me. I got a clock in my stomach.

ANDY: You must have.

BARNEY: I go by that clock, too. Tick, tick. I know it's time for lunch. Tick, tick. I know it's time for dinner. My mother was the same way.

ANDY: I remember that about your mother.

BARNEY: She had a clock in her stomach.

ANDY: Hey, Barn? These clocks you and your mother had in your stomachs—did the ticking keep your father awake at night?

BARNEY: Do you want to get facetious? Do you want to get facetious about the whole thing? Is that what you want to do—get facetious?

ANDY: No, well, I…

BARNEY: Don't get facetious. That happens to be a very common thing, clock in the stomach.

ANDY: I know, I know, I know. Aunt Bee once had an elephant she kept on the mantelpiece and it had a clock in its stomach. Now, don't get mad. I was just kidding.

BARNEY: I don't mind you kidding me about my stomach, but don't kid about my mother's stomach.

ANDY: Well, I wouldn't think of it.

BARNEY: Well, just don't, that's all. Got to draw the line some place, for Pete's sake.

AUNT BEE: *(Entering with tray)* Hello, boys.

ANDY: Oh, hi, Aunt Bee.

AUNT BEE: I'm late. I'm sorry. I had to get my wash hung out. I hope you're not starved.

Aunt Bee's Tuna Fish Sandwiches

1 can (6 ounces) albacore tuna
1/3 cup finely chopped celery
1/4 cup mayonnaise
1 tablespoon olive oil
1 tablespoon fresh lemon juice
Dash paprika
4 slices whole wheat bread
Lettuce
2 little sweet gherkins

Using a fork, combine the first six ingredients in a medium bowl. Spread half of the mixture on two slices of the bread. Top with a lettuce leaf and another piece of bread. Cut the sandwiches in half diagonally. Slice two gherkins in half lengthwise. Place one gherkin half on top of each sandwich half and secure with toothpicks.
Makes 2 sandwiches.

Chocolate Brownies with Walnuts

1/2 cup butter
2 squares unsweetened chocolate
1 cup all-purpose flour, sifted
2 eggs
2 cups sugar
1 teaspoon vanilla extract
1 cup chopped walnuts

Preheat the oven to 350°. Melt the butter and chocolate in a saucepan and let cool. Add the flour, eggs, sugar, vanilla, and walnuts to the chocolate mixture. Pour the mixture into a 9-inch square pan and bake for 35 to 40 minutes. Do not overcook.
Makes 8, plus 1 extra for the taste-tester.

SOMETHING'S BREWING— *When Aunt Bee becomes a lady of leisure, Malcolm Merriweather takes over bringing "high tea" to Andy and Barney.*

Yes sir, this is a lunch:

MALCOLM: Gentleman, a little high tea?

ANDY: Well, what in the world is that?

BARNEY: It looks like a big ravioli.

MALCOLM: It's just a Cornish pasty, that's all.

ANDY: What's a Cornish pasty?

MALCOLM: Well, you see, there's meat and potatoes in one end and plum pudding in the other. So you start with the meat and potatoes and work your way through to the dessert.

ANDY: Well, what do you think of that!

BARNEY: That's something!

ANDY: And salad and pickles, olives.

BARNEY: It's good-bye waistline with you around Malcolm. I'll tell you what…

AUNT BEE: Goodness, you boys won't be satisfied with tuna fish sandwiches, anymore, will you?

ANDY: Whatd'ya say, Aunt Bee?

AUNT BEE: Nothing, nothing.

ANDY: O.K., go ahead and have a good time, Aunt Bee. Boy, is this a lunch? I ask you, is this a lunch?!

BARNEY: Tell me the truth, Malcolm. You used to cook for the king of England, didn't you?

Malcolm's Beef Stew *(with sherry in the gravy)*

6 slices thick bacon
2 pounds beef round, cut into bite-sized cubes
½ cup (double dollop) cooking sherry
½ cup water
2 garlic cloves, chopped
1 teaspoon dried rosemary

1 bay leaf
1 teaspoon salt
Pepper to taste
6 carrots, cut into bite-sized pieces
2 onions, peeled and cut into chunks
8 ounces fresh mushrooms, cleaned and sliced

In a large pot, fry the bacon over medium heat. Remove the bacon and drain on paper towels. Brown the beef in the bacon fat. Remove the beef and pour off most of the liquid fat. (Leave some of the pan scrapings.) Over medium-high temperature, heat the sherry in the same pan. Return the beef to the pot; add the water and seasonings. Bring to a boil, cover, and simmer over low heat for 1 hour, stirring occasionally. Add the bacon, carrots, onions, and mushrooms. Bring the stew to a boil again; then reduce the heat and simmer for about 45 minutes more. Remove the bay leaf and serve.
Serves about 8.

*S*atisfied customer:

ANDY: Mighty good beef stew tonight, Malcolm.
MALCOLM: Oh, well, I'm glad you enjoyed it.
ANDY: Wasn't it good, Aunt Bee?
AUNT BEE: Hmmm?
ANDY: The beef stew Malcolm made.
AUNT BEE: Yes, it was very nice.
BARNEY: Whatd'ya put in that, anyways?
MALCOLM: Oh, that had double dollops of cooking sherry.
BARNEY: Sherry? Well, you shouldn't have done that. I'm on duty tonight.
ANDY: You better chew some gum. It wouldn't do for the duty deputy to go out with gravy on his breath.

For Cornish Pasty, you can't beat Malcolm's very own recipe contributed by Bernard Fox to the cookbook In the Kitchen with Elinor Donahue. *Jolly good!*

Barney and Thelma Lou, Phfftt

CREATURE OF HABIT—*Barney shares his favorite Tuesday night treat.*

A man and his fudge:

BARNEY: Thelma Lou and I have always had a standing date on Tuesday nights. Every Tuesday night for as long as I can remember, we're setting on the couch, a pan of cashew fudge between us, watching that doctor show on TV. Now, all of a sudden, it's slipped her mind.

ANDY: Maybe she wasn't feeling well.

BARNEY: Naah, she was feeling fine. She was humming!

ANDY: Well, like I say, sometimes you can't figure women.

BARNEY: Yeah, you can say that again.

ANDY: Well, I was just fixing to do a little night check up and down Main Street. You wanna come along?

BARNEY: I might as well. I got nothing else to do.

ANDY: Come on.

BARNEY: Want some fudge?

ANDY: You bought some, huh?

BARNEY: Well, a man's had fudge every Tuesday night for years, you don't kick the habit just like that.

ANDY: Yeah.

That Doctor Show Cashew Fudge

1½ cups packed brown sugar
1½ cups granulated sugar
2 teaspoons corn syrup
⅔ cup milk
2 tablespoons butter
½ cup chopped cashews
½ teaspoon vanilla extract

Combine the sugars, corn syrup, milk, and butter in a saucepan. Heat slightly, stirring until the sugar is dissolved. Bring to a boil. Without stirring, boil to the soft ball stage (238°). Remove the pan from the heat and cool gradually. Beat until creamy. Add the nuts and vanilla. Pour the fudge into a buttered pan and spread evenly before it hardens. Cut into squares.
Makes about 1½ pounds.

Back to Nature

LAKE
LOONS—
*Barney
and Gomer
use their
pioneer
moxie to
survive.*

*E*ating on a shoestring budget:

GOMER: I'm about starved. We didn't have no breakfast. It's already past noon.
BARNEY: Well, it won't be long now.
GOMER: But didn't you say you could get food out here in the woods anytime like the pioneers?
BARNEY: Well, sure. Of course I can.

GOMER: Well, if you don't mind, I'd like some of that food off the land and I know that my stomach would appreciate it. That is, if you really can do it.

BARNEY: Well, of course I can do it. Normally I'd just make a snare and catch a pheasant or some such wild bird.

GOMER: Pheasant, huh! Hey that sounds tasty. Let's have that.

BARNEY: Well, I would except you can't make a decent snare without a piece of a string. Boy, if we had a piece of string, I'd catch you a bird dinner you'd never forget. It's just a darn pity…

GOMER: I got some string.

BARNEY: You do?

GOMER: Sure, I always carry an extra shoelace. Here make a snare. Boy, my mouth's already watering for some of that pheasant bird.

Well, what do you know!:

BARNEY: Well, it worked! We caught us a bird. The land is feeding us just like I said!

GOMER: Daniel Boone ain't never done better.

BARNEY: Yeah, Well, it seemed to have cooked up awful fast.

GOMER: Well…

BARNEY: Well, that's easy to understand, though. Any fire started pioneer style's bound to be hotter than fire started from just ordinary matches. You think it's done yet?

A pheasant experience:

BARNEY: There's a taste you can't match with anything you'll ever find in the city, Huh? Even Aunt Bee couldn't have cooked up anything that good.

Wanna bet?

Roasted Chicken as Pheasant

1 3-pound fryer
Salt
1 rib celery, chopped
1 small onion, chopped
Juice of ½ lemon
Butter

Preheat the oven to 325°. Wash and salt the fryer to taste. Stuff the cavity with the celery and onion. Pour the lemon juice over the chicken and dot with butter. Wrap the chicken in foil and place in a pan lined with foil. Bake for 3 hours.
Serves 2 happy campers.

TOO CLOSE FOR COMFORT?—*When Aunt Bee's baby sister and her family come to visit, everybody feels very close. (Of course, things would have been more comfortable if Ollie had remembered his goose-down pillow.)*

Aunt Nora's Mashed Potatoes

10 white potatoes, scrubbed clean and sparingly pared
7 tablespoons butter
1 cup scalded milk
Salt and pepper to taste

Cook the potatoes by boiling in a large, covered pot with about 5 inches of water in the bottom for 30 to 40 minutes. Mash the cooked potatoes with a potato masher until all the lumps are gone. Combine the butter, milk, salt, and pepper in a separate bowl, and gradually blend into the potatoes until the potatoes are fluffy. Serve immediately.
Serves 8.

Barney's Physical

FATTENING UP BARNEY—*"There we are. We will serve our guest first."*—Aunt Bee

*B*arney's yo-yo diet:

THELMA LOU: (*To Barney*) Here's your cake.
ANDY: Hey, you gonna eat all that cake?"
BARNEY: Well, why not?
ANDY: Lot of calories in there.
BARNEY: Well, that's O.K.
ANDY: What do you weigh, anyway?
BARNEY: With or without my gun?
(*Laughs all around the room.*)
ANDY: Without.
BARNEY: Oh, it varies. 138, 138½. I'm up and down.

Barney's about to pop after his first meal of trying to gain weight:
ANDY: You've done fine, Barn.
AUNT BEE: More potatoes, Barney?
(*Barney shakes his head "no."*)
AUNT BEE: Just a little bit more?
(*Barney shakes his head.*)
AUNT BEE: Then I'll get the dessert, banana cream chocolate pie.
BARNEY: (*Shaking his head in pain*) Uhhh…
AUNT BEE: No dessert? Oh, it'd be so helpful. It's nothing but sugar and starch.
ANDY: He's done fine, Aunt Bee. (*Turns to Barney*) I expect you picked up a pound easy.
BARNEY: (*In pain*) I'm gonna go on home.
ANDY: O.K., I'll see you first thing in the morning. Asa's coming over with that contraption. We'll start with the stretching.
BARNEY: Oh, I don't know about that stretching business, Andy. I might end up with a high stomach or something.

Mashed Potatoes

See Aunt Nora's recipe on page 127.

Chopped Steak

1 pound ground beef
1 teaspoon Worcestershire sauce
1 garlic clove, minced
⅛ teaspoon ginger
Dash lemon juice

Mix all of the ingredients together in a large bowl and form into four patties of no more than 1-inch thickness. Place the patties on a broiler pan. Broil for 5 to 7 minutes on each side.
Serves 4.

Rolls

1 cup hot water
1 teaspoon salt
6 tablespoons shortening
¼ cup sugar
1 envelope (¼ ounce) dry yeast
2 tablespoons lukewarm water
1 egg, beaten
4 cups (scant) sifted all-purpose flour, divided

In a large bowl, mix together the first four ingredients. Allow to cool to lukewarm. In a separate bowl, dissolve the yeast in the 2 tablespoons lukewarm water and add the paste to the sugar mixture. Add the egg and 2 cups of the flour, and beat well. Stir in more of the flour until the dough is easy to handle. Shape the dough into balls and place in greased muffin tins. Cover and allow to rise in a warm place until the dough doubles in size (1 to 2 hours). Preheat the oven to 425°. Bake for 10 to 14 minutes. Brush with melted butter.
Makes about 1½ dozen.

Banana Cream Chocolate Pie

1 cup sugar
6 tablespoons all-purpose flour
⅛ teaspoon salt
2 cups scalded milk
2 squares semi-sweet chocolate
3 eggs, separated
1 teaspoon vanilla extract
2 ripe bananas, peeled and sliced
1 baked 9-inch pie shell

In a small bowl, combine ½ cup of the sugar with the flour and salt. Add the milk and stir. Pour into the top of a double boiler and steam for 8 minutes. Add the chocolate squares and continue cooking for 2 more minutes, stirring constantly to make sure the chocolate completely melts. In a separate bowl, beat the egg yolks with ¼ cup of the sugar; then gradually add to the chocolate mixture while stirring constantly. Cook for 5 minutes more in the double boiler and allow to cool. Add the vanilla.

Place half of the bananas in the pie shell and pour in the mixture. Arrange the remaining bananas on top. Make a meringue by beating the egg whites to stiff peaks; then gradually add the remaining ¼ cup of sugar while continuing to beat. Spread meringue on top. Without preheating, place in the oven at 300° and bake for 30 minutes.
Serves 6 to 8.

Double Rich Vanilla Malted
(with Two Raw Eggs)

4 generous scoops French vanilla ice cream
½ cup whole milk
2 raw eggs (*add at your own risk*)
¼ cup whipping cream
2 tablespoons malt

Place all of the ingredients in a blender and blend just until the mixture is of a smooth, thick consistency.
Makes 1 thick, giant shake.

GOOD NOOSE!—*Thelma Lou brings a fattening refreshment for Barney.*

*A*s *Barney stretches in his harness in the closet, Thelma drops by for a visit:*

THELMA LOU: Barney, I brought you something I think you can handle even while you're wearing that thing. Here. (*She hands him the milkshake.*)

BARNEY: Hey, with a straw. I never thought of that. What is it?

THELMA LOU: Double rich vanilla malted with two raw eggs.

BARNEY: (*Taking a swig*) Mmm. Boy, that's thick.

THELMA LOU: Oh, I'm sorry.

BARNEY: No, that's all right. Good practice for puckering, know what I mean?

(*They kiss.*)

THELMA LOU: Oh, Barney, I just know you're gonna make it.

BARNEY: You know, Thel, I'm beginning to think so myself.

THELMA LOU: Well, I gotta run. I'll see you.

BARNEY: O.K.

THELMA LOU: Bye.

(*She absent-mindedly closes the door on Barney.*)

BARNEY: Aaaahh!

SCOUTING BROWNIES—*Opie keeps an eye on the baking progress of Aunt Bee's homemade brownies.*

*A*ll the world's a pan of brownies:

OPIE: How long does it take for brownies?
AUNT BEE: Thirty minutes. Years ago, I was in one of our church plays and I remember my mother and father both saying I was the best one in it.
OPIE: After they come out of the oven, do they have to cool off before we can eat 'em? I like to eat them hot.
AUNT BEE: I even had my name in the church publication. Did I ever show that to you, Opie? Come on, come on. I'll show you.

(They go to the living room.)

OPIE: You going to put some conventionary sugar on them?
AUNT BEE: Confectionery.
OPIE: That's what I meant. Gee, I hope they come out nice and chewy.
AUNT BEE: Now, let's see…There. Here we are. "News from the Altar." Whose name is that playing the role of the Little Princess, hmm?
OPIE: That's your name.
AUNT BEE: So, you see, I *have* been on the stage.
OPIE: Don't you think we oughta be in the kitchen in case they get ready early?
AUNT BEE: I feel certain I could play Lady Mayberry. After all, once you've played the Princess…Wouldn't you say?
OPIE: Huh? Yes, ma'am. I think they're done.
AUNT BEE: They're probably counting on me to do the sewing.
OPIE: I'll get a plate ready.

Little Princess Brownies

½ cup margarine
1½ cups sugar
3 eggs
¾ cup all-purpose flour
1 teaspoon salt
¾ cup cocoa
1 teaspoon vanilla extract

Preheat the oven to 350°. Cream the margarine and sugar. Add the eggs one at a time, beating well after each addition. Add the flour, salt, and cocoa and mix well. Stir in the vanilla extract. The batter will be fairly stiff. Spoon onto a greased and floured 7 x 11-inch brownie pan, or use an 8- or 9-inch square or round pan if you want the brownies to be a bit thicker. Bake for 30 minutes. Cool at least 5 minutes before cutting. Add nuts or frosting at your pleasure. *Makes about 1 dozen.*

Andy and Helen Have Their Day

GOOBER GOBBLES—*There's just no way to load a picnic basket completely full when Goober's around. (And do you think that Andy and Helen had better keep an eye on those sandwiches once they get to their picnic site? Yo!)*

Goober's beholden to grant Andy and Helen their picnic:

GOOBER: Hey, look at all this food.
HELEN: Would you like something, Goober?
GOOBER: Well, maybe just one of them drumsticks.
HELEN: Fine.
GOOBER: You know, Barney says I gotta take very good care of you two. Today could be a very important day for you.
HELEN: What?
ANDY: Uh, nothing. Let's uh…
GOOBER: Boy, I sure love picnics. Hey, remember a movie called *Picnic*?
ANDY: Yeah.
GOOBER: Remember Cary Grant?
ANDY: Cary Grant wasn't in *Picnic*.
GOOBER: He wuddn't? Well, speaking of Cary Grant, I do him, you know.
HELEN: You what?
GOOBER: I take off on Cary Grant. Would you like to hear?
ANDY: Uh, well, Goob, we ought to…
GOOBER: I'd be glad to do it. Cary Grant….Judy, Judy, Judy.
ANDY: Good, Goob. But Cary Grant wasn't in *Picnic*.
HELEN: It was William Holden who was in *Picnic*.
GOOBER: I can't do William Holden. He talks like everybody else.
ANDY: Well, got everything ready here to go.
GOOBER: Sure can't do William Holden, but I can do Cary Grant. Judy, Judy, Judy.
ANDY: Good, Goob.

Drumsticks

Wonderful!

2 pounds chicken legs
¼ cup all-purpose flour
½ teaspoon salt
½ teaspoon paprika
⅛ teaspoon pepper
⅓ cup shortening, melted

Preheat the oven to 425°. Wash and dry the chicken legs. Mix the flour, salt, paprika, and pepper in a paper bag. Put 3 or 4 chicken pieces at a time in the bag and shake to coat with the flour mixture. Place the flour-coated chicken on an ungreased baking pan and drizzle melted shortening on top. Bake for 40 to 45 minutes or until tender.
Serves 4 to 6.

Sandwich Spread

1 pound chopped bologna (or Spam)
2 cups shredded Velveeta cheese
2 hard-boiled eggs, chopped
1 tablespoon grated onion
¾ cup chopped celery
½ cup sweet pickle relish
Mayonnaise to desired consistency

Thoroughly mix together all of the ingredients in a large bowl.
Makes about 5 cups.

Goodbye Dolly

Easy-going Andy gets a Bee sting:

AUNT BEE: Andy, what would you like for supper?

ANDY: Oh, I don't care. Anything you say will be fine.

AUNT BEE: Oh, you know that drives me out of my mind. If you'd only make a suggestion—just once!

Goober Pyle

With the possible exception of Wally, Goober Pyle is Mayberry's top-notch mechanic. Like his cousin Gomer, Goober also enjoys the outdoors and fishing and hunting. A good athlete, he coaches baseball and bowls. Like Gomer before him, Goober can be depended on in a pinch if Mayberry needs an extra deputy. Some of his favorite hobbies are reading (and re-reading) comic books and going to the movies. According to Goober, there are two things he knows: cars and guns. He forgot one other thing: food! He is very likely Mayberry's top eater. And certainly no one else in Mayberry is known to have eaten 57 pancakes in one sitting.

Guest in the House

Andy's flirting with disaster when he and Helen double-date with his "Cousin" Gloria and Goober:

ANDY: There we are.

GLORIA: This is a cute place, Andy.

ANDY: Oh, well, thank you. I'm glad you like it. We come out here often—about once a week. Good food.

GLORIA: Oh.

GOOBER: It's clean, too. They change the tablecloths every night.

GLORIA: Well, what do you recommend, Andy?

ANDY: Well, the special's awful good.

GOOB: Yeah, the special's great.

GLORIA: Well, what is it?

GOOBER: Dollar seventy-five.

ANDY: Uh, it's a pounded steak dinner, Gloria. It's very tasty and tender.

HELEN: I think that's what I'll have.

ANDY: Oh, O.K.

GOOBER: Yeah, I want one.

ANDY: Special? Specials for everybody.

ANDY: (*To the waiter*) We'll have four specials.

FORKING IT OVER— *Or rather under! It's clear that Goober doesn't expect to do much spooning this particular evening.*

Later...:

ANDY: Hey, hey! After supper, why don't we drive over to Mt. Pilot. There's a miniature golf course over there.

GLORIA: Oh, that sounds like fun.

ANDY: Uh, good. We'll do that then? You wanna do that, Helen?

HELEN: That's fine.

(Goober drops his fork on the floor.)

GOOBER: *(To Andy)* Could you reach my fork?

ANDY: Excuse me.

(The men go below the table.)

GOOBER: We can't play miniature golf. Costs a dollar and a quarter.

ANDY: That's for two, Goober.

GOOBER: Well, what about these dinners? I ain't no Rockefeller. I ain't got enough money.

ANDY: I'll pay, I'll pay. Can I get up now?

The blood's rushing to my head.

(Andy and Goober return to the top side of the table.)

ANDY: And then later, if it's not too late, we could take a drive over to the lake and have a nice walk.

GLORIA: Oh.

ANDY: You know where, Helen. Up through the magnolia trees.

HELEN: Oh, yes. It's lovely there.

(Oops! Goober drops his fork again, and he and Andy are back down under for a conference.)

ANDY: What's the matter now? Can't cost you anything to walk.

GOOBER: What am I supposed to do down by the lake—hold her hand, take her arm, or what?

ANDY: Anything you want to do, Goober.

GLORIA: What are you two doing down there, gambling?

(Laughter from all.)

Helen Crump

Miss Crump is Opie's favorite schoolteacher and the lady who wins Andy's heart. She came to Mayberry from her native Kansas. Helen loves teaching, but she also enjoys expressing herself as a writer of children's books. When she can get away from grading homework, she enjoys dancing and going to the movies. (She's a pretty good bowler, too.) Some of her other favorite things to do include going on picnics at Myers' Lake and sharing a special dinner with Andy at Morelli's.

Pounded Steak Dinner

1½ pounds flank steak
Salt and pepper to taste
Flour
2 small potatoes, chopped
1 cup diced carrots
1 onion, chopped
1 rib celery, chopped
2 tablespoons butter
1 cup water

Gravy:
Drippings
Flour
Milk
Salt and pepper, to taste
Worcestershire sauce, to taste

Preheat the oven to 350°. Pound the steak. Sprinkle on some salt and pepper and flour. Pound a little more. Cover the steak with the vegetables; then roll the steak and tie it tightly. In a saucepan, brown the meat in the butter. Transfer the meat to a baking dish, add water, and cover. Bake for about 1 hour or until the meat is tender. Use the drippings to make gravy.

Place the drippings in a skillet over medium heat (being careful not to get it too hot). Combine enough flour and milk to form a thick liquid. (Use a wire whisk to remove any lumps that form.) Slowly add the flour mixture to the drippings while stirring constantly with a whisk. Allow the gravy to bubble, but stir frequently. Add salt, pepper, and Worcestershire sauce to taste. Add flour mixture until you have the thickness desired.
Serves 3 to 4.

Morelli's

When Mayberrians get the urge to eat out and really want something fancy, there's one popular choice—Morelli's. It's on the highway about halfway between Mayberry and Mt. Pilot, but off the road a bit, so it's nice and secluded. It's just right for a romantic night out.

Even Barney, ever the tightwad, will spring for Thelma Lou's dinner every now and then. Well, he did so that one time for her birthday, anyway.

But Morelli's really is a classy place. The waiters are dressed fancy, and the booths have red-and-white checkered tablecloths with candles flickering in used wine bottles. There is latticework with artificial greenery and grapes. The walls are decorated with posters of exotic, faraway locales.

The restaurant is clean too. Goober is especially impressed that they change the tablecloths every night, plus, as he points out, "They got good food and dancing and they've never been raided."

Besides the good food, Morelli's, which is open until 2 A.M. or so, is noted as a great place for dancing with its small but intimate dance floor. There's a jukebox loaded with romantic records for slow dancing, and there's even a gypsy violinist who strolls from booth to booth on certain evenings. (He does appreciate a decent tip, though. Otherwise, he becomes moody.)

Another sign that reflects the elegance of Morelli's is the fact that men usually wear suits and ties when dining there, plus each table has breadsticks (gratis). But the real tip-off that Morelli's is a special place is the fact that they permit the service of wine.

Morelli's specialty is its pounded steak dinner. According to Goober, "The pounded steak dinners are nice. They pound them right here on the premises." With a county-wide reputation of being very tasty and tender, the dish is a bargain at $1.75. There's also the Deluxe Special, which is minestrone and pounded steak à la Morelli for just $1.85.

Barney appreciates the fact that if you're sitting in the right booth, you can look straight into the kitchen and see the chef pounding away on your own personal steak. If you wave at him, he'll more than likely wave right back. (Feel free to send him your compliments.)

And one more thing about Morelli's is that if a case of the late night hungries sneaks up on you and everything is closed in Mayberry, why, you can drive out to Morelli's and get a pizza—pepperoni or mozzarella, your choice. Now that's special.

A Warning from Warren

STRANGE COMBO—*Goober eats his peanut butter and tuna (and ketchup) sandwich and milkshake as he observes Warren tuning in his powers of E.S.P.*

Adventures in eating:

CHARLIE (the Diner Cook): Hamburger *(for Warren)* and peanut butter and tuna *(for guess who)*.
GOOBER: Well, have you got any ketchup? Where's my milkshake?

Warren's Hamburger

2 pounds ground beef
2 eggs
¼ sleeve saltine crackers, crushed
6 large fresh mushrooms, chopped
1 green pepper, chopped

1 onion, chopped
Fresh garlic, minced
Steak spice
Pepper
Barbecue sauce *(optional)*

In a large bowl, mix the first seven ingredients together and pat into burgers—the thicker the better (about ¾ inch thick). Put on the grill and after browning each side for about 5 minutes, shake on steak spice and pepper. Continue to cook until desired doneness. After the last flip of the burgers to each side, brush on a dab of barbecue sauce.
Makes 6 burgers.

Goober's Chocolate Milkshake

3 scoops chocolate ice cream
⅓ cup milk

1½ tablespoons chocolate syrup
⅓ banana *(optional)*

Put all of the ingredients in a blender and mix until smooth or until it's the desired consistency. Pour into a tall glass and dive in.
Serves 1.

We'll do everybody a favor and omit the recipe for Goober's Peanut Butter and Tuna Sandwich

The Cannon

Getting ready for the governor's visit:

FRANK: After the squad car comes the governor's car. Then I want an open convertible with the top down. Who's in charge of transportation?

GOOBER: I am!

FRANK: Think you can take care of that?

GOOBER: Open convertible with the top down?

FRANK: Yeah.

GOOBER: Yeah, I can borrow Earlie Gilley's.

ANDY: Yeah, Earlie will loan you his. What's it for, Frank?

FRANK: Well, I wanted something different. I got to thinking the most important thing we grow around here is potatoes.

ANDY: That's right.

FRANK: So I thought it would be kinda nice if we had our potato queen in the parade.

ANDY: Who is the queen this year?

FRANK: Ol' man Dobbins' daughter.

ANDY: That's right. It's her turn this year.

FRANK: So I thought we'd have a nice crown of potatoes and have her riding in an open convertible in a bathing suit.

AUNT BEE: In a bathing suit, right on Main Street?

ANDY: Oh, yeah, It'll be all right.

ALL EYES ON THE POTATO QUEEN— *The governor is greeted in fine style by Mayberry's reigning Potato Queen.*

Aunt Bee's doing her part of the preparations for the governor:

AUNT BEE:	I think I have the luncheon reception pretty well planned.
ANDY:	Oh, good.
AUNT BEE:	I thought for the first course, I know it's ambitious, but I think the governor'll be impressed.
ANDY:	What?
AUNT BEE:	Shrimp cocktail.
COMMITTEE:	Ohhh.
ANDY:	That's excellent!
AUNT BEE:	Oh, wait, wait. I can't be absolutely certain. I have to check and see whether I can round up any of those fruit cocktail forks. Did you say we're going to have 25 for lunch?
ANDY:	'bout 25.
AUNT BEE:	Well, I thought for the main course we would have Chicken à la King. We girls could prepare it at home and then we would bring it over to the city hall in our big roasting pans.
GOOBER:	That ought to work, Andy.
ANDY:	Yeah, yeah. That'll work.
AUNT BEE:	And for dessert, I thought we'd have ladyfingers and coffee!

Aunt Bee's Shrimp Cocktail and Sauces

See the recipes on page 187.

Chicken à la King Fit for the Governor

1 chicken (3 to 4 pounds)
8 medium onions, sliced
1 teaspoon salt
Dash pepper
1 bay leaf
1/3 cup all-purpose flour
1 cup chicken broth
1/3 cup butter
1½ cups cream
8 ounces fresh mushrooms, sliced
1 six-ounce can pimiento strips

In a pot, simmer the chicken in boiling water with the onions, salt, pepper, and bay leaf. Cool and skim off the fat. Reserve the fat. Strain the broth. Reserve the broth and the onions. Cut the chicken into 1-inch cubes. Liquefy the chicken fat in the top of a double boiler. Sauté the onions in the fat. Sauté the mushrooms in the fat. Add the flour, chicken broth, butter, and cream to the fat, and cook until thickened, stirring constantly. Return the chicken and onions to the mixture. Add the pimientos to the pan. Simmer for 5 minutes, stirring constantly. Serve immediately.
Serves 6.

Since potatoes are Mayberry's top crop, here are a couple of dishes featuring this local favorite:

Bumper Crop Scalloped Potatoes

8 to 10 medium potatoes
2 to 3 medium onions
1 sixteen-ounce carton sour cream
½ cup fresh chives, chopped
1½ cups milk
1½ cups water
⅓ cup margarine
Salt and pepper to taste
Parmesan cheese

Preheat the oven to 400° to 435°. Thinly slice the potatoes and onions and mix with the sour cream, chives, milk, and water in a large bowl. Cut up the margarine and mix in along with salt and pepper to taste. Then place the mixture in a roasting pan and sprinkle Parmesan cheese on top. Bake for approximately 90 minutes (begin checking for doneness at 60 minutes; cooking time will depend on the oven and the thickness of the potatoes).
Serves 8.

Potato Candy

For the times when you've got more potatoes than you know what to do with.
½ cup mashed potatoes
1 teaspoon vanilla extract
Few drops lemon juice
1 pound confectioners' sugar
Peanut butter

Warm the mashed potatoes; while slightly warm, add the vanilla and lemon juice. Stir in the sugar until the mixture is a consistency to roll out. Roll out on waxed paper to ¼-inch thickness. Spread with peanut butter and roll up like a jelly roll. Chill in the refrigerator. Cut into thin slices when ready to serve.
Makes 1½ to 2 pounds.

Ladyfingers

3 egg whites
⅓ cup confectioners' sugar
2 egg yolks
⅓ cup sifted all-purpose flour
⅛ teaspoon salt
½ teaspoon vanilla extract

In a small bowl, beat the egg whites until just stiff. Gradually add the confectioners' sugar while continuing to beat to stiff peaks. In a separate bowl, beat the egg yolks until thick and lemon colored; then fold into the mixture. Sift the flour and salt together in a bowl and add to the eggwhite mixture. Add the vanilla and mix together.

Preheat the oven to 350°. Use a pastry bag to place the dough onto paper covering a cookie sheet in 1-inch-wide fingers of about 4 inches in length. (Opie likes 'em best when they are of varying lengths like real fingers.) Sprinkle with additional confectioners' sugar. Bake for 10 to 12 minutes or until golden brown. Allow to cool slightly; then gently shovel them from the paper onto a wire rack to cool.
Makes about 4 hands worth of fingers, depending on the length of the fingers.

THE HIGHWAY TO A MAN'S STOMACH—*Aunt Bee hopes to drive home her point (and a car) by delighting Andy with some of his favorite foods.*

Aunt Bee's buttering Andy up for something:

OPIE: Pork chops!
ANDY: That's the second time this week. What'd we do to deserve this?
AUNT BEE: Well, I know how fond you are of them.
ANDY: I think I'll just have one here.
OPIE: Here, Pa (*as he passes potatoes*).
ANDY: My, look at that. Well, I guess everybody just dig right in. Mmm, mmm.

Sweet and Sour Pork Chops

1 teaspoon ground ginger
1 teaspoon salt
½ teaspoon pepper
1 teaspoon paprika
¼ cup all-purpose flour

6 pork chops
1 tablespoon salad oil
1 cup pineapple juice
2 tablespoons cider vinegar
3 tablespoons brown sugar

In a large bowl, mix together the ginger, salt, pepper, paprika, and flour. Coat the pork chops in the seasonings. Brown the coated chops in a skillet coated with salad oil. Add the remaining ingredients and cook over low heat for 40 minutes or until the chops are tender.
Serves 3 to 6.

Mashed Potatoes

4 large potatoes, peeled
3 ounces cream cheese, softened
½ cup sour cream

1 teaspoon onion salt
½ teaspoon black pepper
1½ tablespoons butter or margarine

Cook, drain, and mash the potatoes. Add the cream cheese, sour cream, onion salt, pepper, and butter. Beat until fluffy. Cool. Cover and refrigerate. (Can be kept several days.) When ready to eat, place in a greased casserole and dot with butter. Bake at 350° until heated through, about 30 minutes.
Serves 4 to 6.

SPECIAL DELIVERY—*Aunt Bee's got the good cooking in overdrive. Speaking of which, Andy, how about that new car of Aunt Bee's?*

Grilled Corn on the Cob

4 or 5 ears of corn, shucked and cleaned   ¼ cup butter

Wrap the ears of corn in a piece of aluminum foil with ¼ cup of butter. Crimp the foil around the corn and grill until the corn is tender, turning 2 or 3 times.
Serves 4 to 5.

*M*ore buttering up at the courthouse:

AUNT BEE: I brought you lunch.
ANDY: Picnic basket, huh?
AUNT BEE: Pork chops.
ANDY: Pork chops again, for lunch?
AUNT BEE: Well, I know how much you like them.
ANDY: Wow.
AUNT BEE: Beans.
ANDY: Mmm.
AUNT BEE: Chocolate pudding.
ANDY: Chocolate pudding!
AUNT BEE: And some fresh fruit.
ANDY: You've got all my favorites. This is really something.
AUNT BEE: Now, you just enjoy it.
ANDY: Well, I sure will. I'll bring the basket home.
AUNT BEE: Oh no, don't bother. I'll wait.
ANDY: Well, O.K. Mmm, mmm, mmm.
AUNT BEE: Good?
ANDY: Mmmm.

Bee's Beans

1 pound pinto or white dried beans
Salt to taste
Small piece of ham
1 to 2 tablespoons vegetable oil

Wash and soak beans overnight or for 3 to 4 hours. Pour the water off. In a pot, cover with fresh water and salt to taste. Add a small piece of ham and the oil. Cook until tender (about 2 hours) on medium heat. Add water as needed during cooking to make the consistency you like.
Serves 6 to 8.

Sunliner Chocolate Pudding

1½ cups sugar
3 tablespoons cocoa
2 tablespoons self-rising flour
4 egg yolks
1½ cups milk
3 tablespoons butter
1½ teaspoons vanilla extract

In a saucepan, mix together the first three ingredients. Add the egg yolks and mix thoroughly. Add the milk slowly while stirring. Bring to a boil over medium heat. Take off the heat and stir in the butter and vanilla.
Serves 4 to 6.

PLATE-CROSSED LOVERS—*Flora shows her favoritism by who gets the bigger serving of meat loaf.*

*S*o that's *what happened to the clock in Barney's stomach:*

GOOBER: Want to go over to the Diner and have lunch?
ANDY: O.K....
GOOBER: If you don't get to the Diner early enough all the good desserts are gone.
ANDY: Yeah.
GOOBER: And they sure do have good mashed potatoes. Best in Mayberry, don't you think so, Andy?
ANDY: Yeah, they're pretty good.
GOOBER: If you get there too late they get lumpy.

Easy ordering:
ANDY: I'll have the meat loaf plate.
GOOBER: Me too.
ANDY: That'll be two meat loaf plates.
FLORA: Coming up.

Later...:
GOOBER: I can tell she likes me, Andy. Look at all the meat loaf she give you just because you're a friend of mine.

Diner Mashed Potatoes

8 small white potatoes
1 garlic clove, minced
1 teaspoon olive oil
½ cup milk
6 tablespoons butter

¼ cup sour cream
2 ounces cream cheese
¼ teaspoon paprika
Salt and black pepper to taste

Preheat the oven to 450°. Bake the potatoes until tender (about 40 minutes). When the potatoes are almost done, sauté the minced garlic in the olive oil in a saucepan. Lightly brush the potatoes with the garlic paste. Mash the potatoes with a potato masher. In the saucepan, combine the milk, butter, sour cream, cream cheese, paprika, and salt and black pepper. Heat and stir until a smooth sauce is formed. Blend the cream sauce with the potatoes and serve hot with Diner Meat Loaf and bread to complete Goober's favorite Meat Loaf Plate.
Serves 6 to 8.

FLORA
ARRANGEMENT—
*"Flora, you sure do set a
nice desk."*—Goober

Diner Meat Loaf

1 pound lean ground beef or ground chuck
1 can (10¾ ounces) vegetable soup
1 egg

3 slices bread, dried and crumbled
½ onion, chopped
Pepper to taste

Preheat the oven to 350°. In a large bowl, mix all of the ingredients and place in a 9-inch-square pan and flatten. Bake for 30 to 35 minutes or until done. Serve with mashed potatoes and carrots.
Serves 6.

Diner Pot Roast

3 to 4 pounds beef round
1 onion, sliced
3 strips bacon
½ teaspoon ground ginger

3 tomatoes, cut into thirds
½ cup grated carrot
1 green pepper, quartered
Salt and pepper to taste

Tie the meat together with string. Brown the onion and bacon together in a heavy pot. Add the meat and sear it on all sides. Add the ginger, tomatoes, carrot, and green pepper. Add 2 cups of water and bring to a boil; then cover and simmer for 1 hour; add water while cooking, if necessary. Add salt and pepper to taste. Simmer for 1 hour more, or until the meat is good and tender. Serve with Diner Mashed Potatoes and a roll to make the Pot Roast Plate. (Use the drippings as gravy.)
Serves 6 to 8.

The battle lines are drawn at the Diner:

FLORA: Well, at least have a piece of pie. We have fresh blueberry pie and the peach is simply fantastic and the apple is real yummy.

ANDY: O.K., apple. (*To Helen*) Want a piece of pie?

HELEN: Fine.

ANDY: What kind?

HELEN: Oh, whichever one's the yummy one.

Ready, aim, fire…:

FLORA: Are you coming up for lunch tomorrow, Andy? We're having chicken à la king and it's real delish.

ANDY: I don't think so, Flora.

HELEN: Andy, how could you pass up something that's going to be so delish. I wouldn't be surprised if the bread pudding wasn't absolutely fab.

Even though Flora says the Diner's Chicken à la King is "delish," Andy passes on it. He prefers Aunt Bee's recipe (see page 144).

And since Andy and Helen both pass on the peach and blueberry pies in favor of—what else?—the apple one, we'll make the same choice.

Diner Apple Pie

Two-layer 9-inch pie crust
6 cups Granny Smith apples, peeled, scored, and sliced (about 8)
1 teaspoon lemon juice
½ teaspoon lemon zest
1 cup sugar
2 tablespoons all-purpose flour
½ teaspoon allspice
½ teaspoon ground cinnamon
Pinch salt

Preheat the oven to 400°. Place the bottom crust in the pie plate. Coat the sliced apples with the lemon juice and zest. In a large bowl, combine the dry ingredients; then toss the apples in the mixture. Place the apples evenly on top of the pastry. Cover with the top crust and flute the edges. Cut vents in the top and bake for 50 to 60 minutes. (If the pastry begins to brown too much, cover the edges with aluminum foil.) Serve hot with vanilla ice cream.
Makes 6 Andy-sized servings or 10 Helen-sized servings.

The Gypsies

BLUE SKIES FROM NOW ON—*Shortly after the dry-witted gypsies put a drought curse on Mayberry, the Taylors and Helen enjoy a meal with vegetables apparently brought in from places with more rainfall.*

Tomato Salad

3 large tomatoes, chopped
1 medium cucumber, peeled and chopped
1 medium onion, chopped
1 medium green pepper, chopped

Salt and pepper, to taste
1 cup corn oil
½ cup wine vinegar
2 tablespoons sugar

In a large bowl, combine the vegetables. Add salt and pepper. In a separate bowl, mix the corn oil, wine vinegar, and sugar. Pour over the vegetables and marinate for 1 hour or more. Drain to serve.
Serves 4.

*E*verybody complains about the weather:

ANDY: Mmm, mmm! Good tomatoes, Aunt Bee.
AUNT BEE: Hmm. You know how much they cost?
ANDY: Uh-mm.
AUNT BEE: Forty-three cents a pound.
(Andy whistles in amazement.)
AUNT BEE: It's this dry spell we're having. The tomato crops haven't done very well around here. The longer it doesn't rain, the more expensive they'll get.
HELEN: I guess they shipped these in from Mexico.
OPIE: It must be raining down there.
ANDY: Probably.

HERE COMES THE PITCH—*Clara and Aunt Bee have fed Keevy Hazelton a nice meal, they've got him cornered on the couch, and they're about to knock him out with their "My Hometown" song. (Well, O.K., so what if Keevy falls asleep in the recliner half way through the audition. It just goes to show that it's a very relaxing song.)*

Pot roast payola:

AUNT BEE: Clara, why don't we ask him over?
ANDY: Who over?
CLARA: Maybe for dinner.
ANDY: Who for dinner?
AUNT BEE: Yes, I'll make a pot roast.
CLARA: Yes, tonight.
ANDY: A pot roast for who?
AUNT BEE: Keevy Hazelton. We're going to ask him to sing our song on TV.

Pot Roast

¼ cup vegetable oil
3- or 4-pound rump roast
1 cup water

1 small package dry onion soup mix
1 can (10¾ ounces) cream of mushroom soup

In a black iron skillet, heat the oil and sear the roast on all sides until brown. Remove from the skillet, add the water, soup mix, and mushroom soup to the skillet. Stir over low heat until thoroughly mixed. Place the roast in a Crock-Pot and pour the soup mixture over the roast. Cover and cook on LOW for 10 to 12 hours or on HIGH for 5 to 6 hours. Let cool somewhat before carving. Add a flour-water mixture to the juices for gravy.
Serves 6 to 8.

The Darling Fortune

COLORFUL CHARACTERS— *Full of personality, the Darling boys* (left to right: *Dean, Rodney, Doug, and Mitch with his chiseled features) light up the Taylor porch while visiting with Aunt Bee, Briscoe, and Charlene.*

The Darling family has come in to a $300 fortune:

ANDY: You know what? With all that's happening to the Darling family, we ought to have a celebration.

BRISCOE: If you're talking about some of Miss Bee's cooking, you're on.

ANDY: I'll tell you what. I'll go in there and call her and you meet me at my house at twelve o'clock.

BRISCOE: Good, that'll give me time to get the boys curried up.

Good Taters

½ pound thick bacon
1 onion, sliced
6 medium potatoes, sliced into ¼-inch slices
Salt and pepper
½ teaspoon Worcestershire sauce
1 cup milk
¼ cup butter, melted
1 cup grated Cheddar cheese

Cut the bacon into 1-inch pieces and fry in a skillet over medium heat until crisp. Remove, drain on paper towels, and set aside. Sauté the onions in the drippings. Remove about half of the onions. Place about half of the potatoes on top of the onions in the skillet. Sprinkle on a pinch of pepper. Add the rest of the onions, then the rest of the potatoes. Add the Worcestershire sauce and salt and pepper to taste. Pour the milk and then the melted butter over the potatoes. Sprinkle the bacon on top and heat until boiling. Reduce the heat and simmer, covered, for 30 minutes or until the potatoes are tender. During the last 10 minutes top with the grated cheese.
Makes about 4 servings.

Bee's Black-Eyed Peas

1 pound dried black-eyed peas
2 medium smoked ham hocks
½ teaspoon salt
1 teaspoon black pepper
1 pinch baking soda
1 medium onion, chopped

Wash and sort the peas. Wash the ham hocks and place in a pot with cold water. Boil the meat about 1½ hours or until the pork is tender. Place the peas and other ingredients in the pot. Boil until the peas are tender to the touch (about 1 hour). Serve with cornbread, sliced tomatoes, and onions.
Serves 4.

Chompin' Steak

4 pounds steak
1 lemon, thinly sliced
3 tablespoons butter
1 cup ketchup
1 tablespoon salt
1 teaspoon dry mustard
½ teaspoon pepper
1 teaspoon Worcestershire sauce
2 onions, sliced
½ cup water

Preheat the oven to 350°. Combine all of the ingredients in a large ovenproof pot. Cover and bake for 2 hours or until good and tender.
Serves 8 hearty eaters.

Briscoe's Favorite Blueberry Muffins

¾ cup all-purpose flour
¾ cup whole wheat flour
½ cup (*generous*) brown sugar
1 teaspoon baking powder
½ teaspoon salt
1 egg, beaten

½ cup milk
½ cup melted butter
1½ cups blueberries
½ teaspoon lemon juice
⅛ teaspoon vanilla extract
¼ cup confectioners' sugar

Preheat the oven to 400°. In a medium bowl, mix together the flours, brown sugar, baking powder, and salt. Briskly stir in the egg. Add the milk and butter, and mix well. Rinse the blueberries, sprinkle with the lemon juice and vanilla, and gently stir. Roll the berries in the confectioners' sugar. Gently fold the berries into the batter. Pour the batter into 12 greased muffin cups. Bake for 20 minutes.
Makes 12.

REEL MEN—*Andy and Opie try their luck at snagging Old Sam, one of the few fish with the wits to elude Andy's good old Eagle-Eye Annie.*

CATCH OF THE DAY— *Howard snags the legendary Old Sam, but this is one fish that won't end up in a frying pan.*

*A*t least Howard won't starve on his first day of fishing:

ANDY: Well, better go. Grab the sandwiches. You did bring something to eat?
HOWARD: Oh, yes. Two roast chickens, a quart of potato salad, and lemon pie.
ANDY: Good.

Later…:

NEWSPAPERMAN: I suppose you realize, Mr. Sprague, that catching what is almost a legendary fish is quite a story?
HOWARD: Oh, yeah, yeah. I consider it a triumph of science over animal cunning.
NEWSPAPERMAN: What kind of bait did you use, Mr. Sprague?
HOWARD: Well, now that's an interesting point. I had been using a variety of complicated lures, but after lunch I had some potato salad left, and that's what got him.

Cold Potato Salad

7 to 8 potatoes
1 onion, chopped
4 hard-boiled eggs

6 to 8 ounces of dill relish
1 tablespoon mustard
Miracle Whip

Peel, cube, and boil the potatoes. Add the other ingredients and mix together. Put enough Miracle Whip in to make the salad creamy (about ½ cup). Refrigerate before serving.
Serves 6 to 8.

The Ball Game

HOME-PLATE—*What was supposed to be a luncheon celebrating victory by the Mayberry Giants has taken a gloomy slide after Andy calls Opie out at home. (This is a meal that the Taylors probably don't like to dwell on, so we'll just move on to a more triumphant occasion.)*

A New Doctor in Town

DINNER IS SERVED—*A feast to welcome the new doctor to town.*

Time to gobble:

ANDY:	(*At table*) Hey, I smell something good. I bet it's your turkey.
AUNT BEE:	Ohhh, it should be done by now…Here we are.
ANDY:	Would you look at that? Is that not beautiful? What'll it be? White meat or dark?
AUNT BEE:	Oh…sweet potatoes. They're in the oven.

Making the cut:

OPIE:	Boy, am I hungry.
AUNT BEE:	Well then, why don't we start? Would anyone like to do the carving? Dr. Peterson, would you care to do the honors?
DR. PETERSON:	Well, thank you. I'd be happy to.
FLOYD:	Well, if anyone should know about carving it should be a doctor.

Later…:

CLARA:	Did you see him try to carve that turkey?
FLOYD:	A man on an operating table wouldn't have had a chance.

Still later…:

FLOYD:	You cannot judge a doctor by the way he carves a turkey. Ha!

Sweet Potato Casserole

Casserole:
1 cup shredded coconut
⅓ cup all-purpose flour
1 can (40 ounces) sweet potatoes, drained
  and mashed
1 cup sugar
⅓ cup butter
2 eggs
1 teaspoon vanilla extract

Topping:
1 cup brown sugar
⅓ cup butter, melted
1 cup nuts

Preheat the oven to 350°. In a large bowl, combine all the ingredients except for the topping. Pour into a buttered 9 x 12-inch baking dish. In a small bowl, combine the topping ingredients and spread over the casserole. Bake for 30 minutes.
Serves 8 to 10.

Turkey

14- to 16-pound turkey
Salt and pepper
Water

Remove the giblets and neck from the turkey cavity. Rinse the turkey with cold running water and drain well. If you want to add stuffing, lightly stuff the cavity and fold the skin over. Skewer closed if necessary. Preheat the oven to 325°. Place the turkey, breast side up, in a large roasting pan. Put half an inch of water in the pan. Rub the turkey all over with salt and pepper. Insert a meat thermometer into the thickest part of the thigh next to the body—make sure that the end does not touch bone. Roast the turkey for 15 minutes per pound (approximately 3½ to 4 hours for a 14- to 16- pound turkey). The turkey is done when the thigh temperature reaches 180° to 185°. During cooking, the turkey will brown fairly quickly, so cover the wings and drumsticks with foil part way through baking. If the breast looks too brown, you may also cover it loosely with foil.
Serves 6 to 8.

Malcolm at the Crossroads

FIGHTING IRISH AND THE GENTLEMAN'S ENGLISH—*"I dropped by to invite you up to my cave to eat. Got some possum steak, nice and tender. Been beatin' at 'em with a stick. Ain't nothing too good for my bosom pal."—Ernest T. Bass*

Dinner at Eight

BE
PREPARED—
*Andy explains
to Opie the
importance of
eating all of
the food on
his plate.*

Mark these words (they'll come in handy later):

OPIE: I'm all ready.

ANDY: What do you mean you're all ready? You've barely touched your breakfast.

OPIE: Well, I don't think I ought to eat too much with a long hike ahead of me.

ANDY: Eat.

AUNT BEE: That's when you need it most, Opie—when you're burning up your vitamins.

OPIE: But I'm just not very hungry, Pa.

ANDY: The only excuse for not eating at mealtimes is when you're sick.

OPIE: Well, I'm not sick, but gee, Pa...

ANDY: We don't waste food around here. When something's served to you, you eat. Now, there's a lot of people in this world that would give anything to sit down to a meal like that, so you go ahead.

If a man does not keep pace with his fellow grocery shoppers…:

HOWARD: Hey, Andy, heh-heh-heh!

ANDY: Oh, hi, Howard. How's it coming?

HOWARD: Oh, fine, fine.

ANDY: Good, good, good, good.

HOWARD: Hey, I see you've been doing a little shopping.

ANDY: Oh, yeah. Yeah, yeah, yeah. Wild mushrooms, canned oysters and chili sauce, pickled avocados, chocolate syrup, shrimp enchiladas.

HOWARD: That's a rather unusual assortment, isn't it?

ANDY: Does kind of have a bounce to it, doesn't it?

HOWARD: Heh-heh-heh.

ANDY: You going in, are you?

HOWARD: Oh, yeah. Mother wants (*reading his list*) oatmeal, two quarts whole milk, a dozen brown eggs, a container of yogurt, three dozen oranges.

ANDY: Yeah.

HOWARD: Mother likes me to get plenty of vitamin C during the flu season.

ANDY: That's very, very good thinking. Well…

HOWARD: Oh, Andy, may I ask you a rather personal question?

ANDY: Shoot.

HOWARD: Do you usually eat things like oysters and chocolate syrup and shrimp enchiladas?

ANDY: No-no-no-no-no. See, uh, Aunt Bee is out of town. She's visiting her sister in Raleigh, Opie's on a camping trip, and so I'm, uh, batching it.

HOWARD: You mean all alone?

ANDY: All alone. And I'm really looking forward to it, too. I eat anything I want to eat, do anything I want to do. If I feel like walking right in the living room, taking my shoes off, walking around in my stocking feet, well…

HOWARD: You mean you'd actually leave your shoes right in the middle of the living room floor.

ANDY: If I wanted to.

HOWARD: Gosh….Well, I'd better be going before Mother thinks I've had an accident with the eggs.

ANDY: Yeah, stay right with it, Howard.

HOWARD: See you, Andy.

Wild Mushrooms

¼ cup chicken broth
1 pound large mushrooms, cut into quarters
½ small onion, chopped
2 garlic cloves, minced
2 teaspoons oregano
Black pepper

Pour the chicken broth into a lightly sprayed, non-stick skillet. Add the mushrooms, onion, and garlic. Cook over medium-high heat for about 5 minutes. Add oregano and pepper to taste. Cook, stirring occasionally, until the liquid is absorbed.
Serves 4.

Canned Oysters

2 cans oysters
Soda crackers
4 to 5 hard-boiled eggs
½ cup margarine
Milk

Preheat the oven to 350°. Drain the oysters. Pour 1 can of oysters into a casserole. Cover with a layer of cracker crumbs, then with a layer of sliced eggs. Repeat. Slice the margarine and put on top. Pour milk to cover the mixture and bake until it bubbles and browns (about 20 minutes). If the mixture is dry, add a small amount of milk and reheat.
Serves 4.

Chili Sauce

2 quarts chopped tomatoes
1 cup chopped celery
2 cups chopped apples
1 cup chopped onion
2 green peppers
1 banana pepper, chopped
1 teaspoon salt
2½ cups sugar
1 cup vinegar
1 teaspoon pickling spice

Cook all of the ingredients over medium heat in a large pot until thick (about 3 to 4 hours). Seal in hot sterilized jars.
Makes about 4 quart jars.

Pickled Avocados

1½ cups sugar
¾ cup vinegar
1 cup water
4 cups sliced avocados

Mix the sugar, vinegar, and water in a saucepan. Heat to boiling, stirring often. In a large bowl, pour over the avocados and cool. Cover and refrigerate at least 8 hours.
Serves 4.

THE BEST-LAID PLANS— *Spaghetti with Goober wasn't what Andy originally had in mind for his supper, but when it's good food with a good friend, well, why not enjoy it.*

A Goob man is hard to find:

GOOBER: Guess what I'm cooking for our supper. Guess!…Spaghetti. With my own secret spaghetti sauce.

ANDY: Goob, listen, listen. This is very thoughtful of you and I'd love to have you move in with me and cook for me and everything, but I can't let you put yourself out this way.

GOOBER: You might as well save your breath, Andy. I ain't taking no for an answer.

ANDY: I'll see you.

GOOBER: Well, where you going?

ANDY: To the office, to the office.

GOOBER: What you going there for?

ANDY: Paperwork, Goob, just some paperwork.

GOOBER: Andy, while you're doing your paperwork, guess what I'm going to be doing.

ANDY: I don't know, Goob.

GOOBER: Making the spaghetti sauce.

ANDY: Fine, Goob, fine.

Chocolate Syrup

½ cup margarine
¼ cup milk
¼ cup cocoa
1 cup sugar

Melt the margarine in a saucepan. Blend in the remaining ingredients with a wire whisk. Bring the sauce to a boil. Boil for just 1 minute without stirring. Serve over ice cream (or shrimp enchiladas, if you're making yourself a bachelor meal).
Makes about 1 cup.

Shrimp Enchiladas

1 pound popcorn shrimp
1 tablespoon margarine
1 teaspoon salt
2 garlic cloves, minced
¼ cup onion, chopped
1 can (10¾ ounces) cream of shrimp soup
¾ can (8 ounces) evaporated milk
½ pound Velveeta cheese
1 package (8 ounce) green onion dip
1 small can (4 ounces) green chilies
1 small can (2 ounces) chopped pimiento
½ pound Longhorn cheese (*grated*)
Corn tortillas, softened

In a saucepan, sauté the shrimp in margarine with the salt, garlic, and onion. Then heat the soup, milk, Velveeta cheese, onion dip, chilies, and pimiento in a double boiler. Add the Longhorn cheese to the shrimp. Preheat the oven to 350°. Roll the shrimp and Longhorn cheese mixture into the softened corn tortillas. Line an 8 x 12-inch pan with the enchiladas, and then pour the sauce over the top. Bake for 45 minutes.
Makes about 6.

Goober's Spaghetti Sauce

2 pounds ground round steak
2 green peppers, chopped
2 large onions, chopped
2 ribs celery, chopped
2 cans (16 ounces each) whole tomatoes
2 cans (6 ounces each) tomato paste
2 garlic cloves, minced
2 bay leaves
Oregano to taste
Dash Worcestershire sauce
½ teaspoon mustard seed
1 tablespoon parsley flakes
Salt and pepper to taste
1 cup sliced mushrooms

Cook the first four ingredients in a large pot until the meat is browned. Drain off the excess fat. Add the remaining ingredients. Reduce the heat, cover, and simmer for 2 to 3 hours. Stir occasionally. Serve over generous helpings of spaghetti noodles.
Serves 8.

Later...:

ANDY: Mmm, mmm, mmm. You know, Goob, this *is* good spaghetti sauce. Real good!
GOOBER: I knew you'd like it. Have some more.
ANDY: Mmm...just a little bit...There we are.
GOOBER: It's all in the special sauce—my very own secret sauce.
ANDY: Oh, a secret, huh? Did you make it up out of your own head?
GOOBER: It's a family hand-me-down with a secret ingredient so it won't do you any good to ask
          what it is.
ANDY: O.K., I won't.
GOOBER: Oregano.
ANDY: Huh?
GOOBER: You mix in something called oregano.
ANDY: Oh, oregano. Ohhh, that's the secret ingredient?
GOOBER: Yeah.
ANDY: Mmm, good!

Goober gives Andy a phone message about dinner with the Spragues and...

HOWARD: Mother! Mother! It's Andy Taylor and somehow he has the idea he's been invited
                   to dinner!
MRS. SPRAGUE: Dinner!
HOWARD: Yes.
MRS. SPRAGUE: Tonight!
HOWARD: Yes!
MRS. SPRAGUE: Where in the world did he get an idea like that?!
HOWARD: I don't know. I saw him at the grocery store this morning, and later I called and
                   left a message that the young people's meeting had been changed, but I never
                   mentioned a word about dinner.
MRS. SPRAGUE: Oh dear! You must have said something.
HOWARD: No, no! I didn't say anything. Well, well, what...what are we going to do?
MRS. SPRAGUE: Well, thank heavens we have plenty of leftovers. Now, you go set the table for
                   three while I get things started in here.
HOWARD: Three?!
MRS. SPRAGUE: Yes, three. If Andrew thinks he's been invited for dinner, we can't very well let
                   him eat alone. Now, go.

THE MOTHER OF ALL SPAGHETTI DINNERS—*Andrew devours Mrs. Sprague's old family recipe.*

Sprague Family Spaghetti Sauce

½ pound ground beef
1 small onion, chopped
2 garlic cloves, minced
1 teaspoon dried oregano
1 jar (15 ounces) tomato sauce
1 can (14½ ounces) whole tomatoes, chopped
1 teaspoon dried parsley

In a skillet, cook the beef, onion, and garlic over medium heat until brown. Drain off the excess fat. Add the remaining ingredients, cover, and simmer, stirring occasionally, for 1 hour. *Serves 4.*

*D*inner with the Spragues—heh-heh-heh-cup:

ANDY: This certainly is delicious spaghetti, Mrs. Sprague—especially that sauce of yours.

MRS. SPRAGUE: Oh, thank you, Andrew. It's something of a secret recipe—handed down through five generations of the Sprague family.

ANDY: Oh, a secret? Oh, well, whatever it is in there, it certainly is tantalizing.

MRS. SPRAGUE: I really shouldn't tell you, Andrew, but it's a Greek spice called…oregano.

ANDY: Oh-oh. Well, who in the world would think of putting oregano in a sauce.

HOWARD: That's what makes it a *secret* recipe, Andy.

ANDY: Oh, I guess it would, wouldn't it?

MRS. SPRAGUE: Oh, Andrew, your plate's almost empty *(She gives him more spaghetti.)*

ANDY: Oh, really, I couldn't.

Later back at home, where the shrimp enchiladas have long since missed their chance:

GOOBER: I remember now. It was Howard that called about the young people's meeting and Helen who called…I guess you know that already.

ANDY: Yes, I know that already. Now, I'm going over to Helen's and eat my third supper. And then I'm coming home and I'm gonna kill you.

UH-OH, SPAGHETTI OHHH'S!— *Ding-Ding, Round Three and Andy's about to be down for the count!*

Uncle Edward's Spaghetti Sauce

Oh, you can eat just a wheedle more, can't you?

2 pounds ground beef
1 medium onion, finely chopped
1 green pepper, finely chopped
2 cans (15 ounces each) tomato sauce
2 cans (12 ounces each) tomato paste
1 teaspoon chili powder

3 cups water
1 tablespoon sugar
1 teaspoon oregano leaves, chopped
2 garlic cloves, crushed
1 bay leaf

In a large skillet, cook the ground beef until half-browned and drain off the excess fat. Add the onion and green pepper and continue cooking until the beef is browned and the onion is tender. (Do not drain off any more of the fat.) Add the remaining ingredients. Cover and simmer for 1½ hours, stirring periodically. Serve over 1 pound of cooked spaghetti and top with Parmesan cheese.
Serves 8.

Andy cries "Uncle" as he embarks on his third supper:

ANDY: Well, what do you know—spaghetti!

HELEN: Well, I can't take credit for the entire meal. Uncle Edward supervised the sauce.

UNCLE
EDWARD: Yeah, I got the recipe from a famous Italian chef in New York City.

ANDY: Is that right?

UNCLE
EDWARD: Yeah, it took me all evening to wheedle it out of him.

ANDY: Bet it did.

UNCLE
EDWARD: You're not kidding. But I used my wits. Actually, it all centers around one secret ingredient…

ANDY: Oregano.

UNCLE
EDWARD: (*Disappointed*) Yeah. How do you know?

ANDY: (*Embarrassed*) I guessed.

HELEN: Is something the matter, Andy?

ANDY: Oh, no. It looks like delicious spaghetti. But, uh, the fact is, uh, I'm on a diet.

HELEN: Well, when did that start?

ANDY: Well, I've been thinking about it for just weeks. But, boy, mmm, mmm, that Italian chef really knew what he was talking about.

UNCLE
EDWARD: I told you, didn't I. Come on, Andy, now dig in, dig in.

ANDY: Dig in, dig right in. Yes sir, mmm.

If only Opie's rained-out camping trip had been in India:

HELEN: Now, you just sit there and eat till your heart's content.

OPIE: Boy, spaghetti ! I love spaghetti!

HELEN: Well, your father doesn't seem to care for his.

ANDY: Well, a diet is a diet.

UNCLE
EDWARD: (*Chortling*) Well, what you need is more sauce, sakes aland.

OPIE: You mean you're going to leave all that food on your plate, Pa?

ANDY: Well, uh.

OPIE: What about what you told me this morning?

ANDY: What was that?

OPIE: You know, about all the people in the world not having enough to eat and how it's almost a crime for us not to finish everything on our plate.

ANDY: Well, Ope, there are extenuating circumstances.

OPIE: I even told our scoutmaster what you said, and he said that if more people felt that way, it would be a better world.

ANDY: He's a fine man.

OPIE: If this food weren't here, it might be in India, so we should eat it and not let it go to waste.

ANDY: Well, Ope…

HELEN: Eat.

ANDY: What?

HELEN: Eat!

ANDY: Mmm, good.

Aunt Bee's Restaurant

A versatile chef makes the transition from the Spare Ribs Tavern to Aunt Bee's Canton Palace, just like that:

AUNT BEE: You're an excellent chef.

CHARLIE: Medium, medium. Spare ribs kinda tricky.

AUNT BEE: What are you going to do now, Charlie?

CHARLIE: Go back to Pittsburgh. Wong Su's Canton Palace. Always got a job there. That's what they should have opened here in Mayberry. Chinese restaurant. Big smash. Gold mine.

AUNT BEE: Well, that's very interesting, Charlie. Why don't you open up one here? Right on this very spot. I assume you know how to cook Chinese dishes.

CHARLIE: Are you kidding? Ever since I was seventeen. Chop suey, chow mein, eggrolls, all that jazz. The problem is money. It'd take a lot of money to fix up the place—Chinese Lanterns, Chinese screens, Chinese soup bowls, and those crazy little spoons. Ah, but everything cost money.

AUNT BEE: But why don't you try to find a partner. You have the know-how. He can put up the money.

CHARLIE: Sure, sure. Where do I find a partner? Not a chance. Pittsburgh, here I come.

AUNT BEE: Well, I'll make it a point to ask about.

Everybody's lucky day:
AUNT BEE: Andy, I'm going into the Chinese restaurant business.

ANDY: What?

AUNT BEE: It can be a gold mine. It can be a smash.

Seeking a second opinion:
ANDY: What do you think of a Chinese restaurant here in Mayberry?

HOWARD: Well, personally, I've always been partial to oriental cuisine. I'm especially fond of those little water chestnuts that are so much a part of their main diet.

Order up:
ANDY: You're on, Goob.

GOOBER: I'll have the dollar sixty-five chow mein dinner.

ANDY: I'm buying.

GOOBER: Dollar ninety-five!

Dollar Ninety-Five Chow Mein Dinner

1 cup finely chopped celery
1 medium onion, chopped
Butter
2 cans (10¾ ounces each) cream of mushroom soup
1 jar (6 ounces) sliced mushrooms
⅔ cup unsalted cashews
2 whole chicken breasts, cooked, skinned, and cubed
Chow mein noodles

Preheat the oven to 350°. In a large saucepan, sauté the celery and onion in a little butter until the celery is mostly cooked. Cook the onion until transparent. Add the undiluted mushroom soup, mushrooms, cashews, and chicken. Mix well and pour into a casserole dish. (The casserole can be frozen at this point.) Bake uncovered for 45 minutes. Take out of the oven and add ¾ of the noodles. Mix and cook for 10 more minutes. Put the remaining noodles on top and cook for 5 more minutes.
Serves 4 to 6.

*E*ast coasters:

HOWARD: Aunt Bee certainly has fixed it up attractively with all the lanterns and screens and everything.

GOOBER: Yeah, if you didn't know where you were, you'd think you was right in the heart of Tokyo.

ANDY: Or near there, anyway.

"E" before "N" in "Chicken" and "Chi" before "Chi" in "Ling Chi Chi" ("I always forget that rule"):

AUNT BEE: How did the printers make out with the menu?

CHARLIE: I'm checking those now. He spell some things wrong, but nobody know the difference.

AUNT BEE: I'm not so sure.

CHARLIE: It's nothing. Ling chi chi. That means chicken. He left out one chi. So what? You know what I mean?

AUNT BEE: Uh-huh, I suppose so.

There's one in every crowd:

ANDY: What are you going to have, Helen?

HELEN: Gee, I dunno yet. Everything looks so intriguing.

ANDY: Yeah.

HOWARD: I think for the main course I'm gonna have the chicken. That's down here, ling chi chi. Oh, they left the chi off.

GOOBER: You're really an expert on this stuff, ain't you, Howard?

HOWARD: Well.

Charlie Lee's Ling Chi Chi

Brought to Mayberry via Pittsburgh.

1 pound chicken breasts (cooked and cut into thin strips)
1 tablespoon vegetable oil
3 tablespoons soy sauce
1 teaspoon garlic powder
1 cup water
16 ounces frozen mixed vegetables
    (broccoli, carrots, peppers, etc.)
4 cups cooked rice

Added 1 T sesame oil

I added chopped onion

In a large skillet, cook the chicken quickly in vegetable oil over medium high heat. In a bowl, mix the soy sauce and garlic powder with the water and pour over the chicken. Add the vegetables and cook until done. Serve over cooked rice.
Serves 3 to 4.

Goob Fortune:

GOOBER: Hey, do we get them fortune cookies here?

ANDY: Oh yeah, with dessert.

GOOBER: I'm anxious to see what mine is. Maybe it'll say I'm gonna be a millionaire.

HOWARD: Yeah, they have some very interesting prognostications in there. I get a big bang out of them.

Howard Sprague

County clerk Howard Sprague is the consummate civil servant, one who takes his public duties quite seriously. Howard, a cautious soul, lives many of his adult years with his mother. He enjoys fellowship with Andy, Goober, and Emmett. He was thrilled the day he gained entrance into the Regal Order of the Golden Door to Good Fellowship. A big reader, Howard is also a part-time writer for the *Mayberry Gazette,* for which he covers everything from gardening to, in a pinch, Little League baseball. As for food, his tastes in cuisine lean to the exotic, such as Morelli's or Ching Lee's in Mt. Pilot. But there's nothing outlandish about his character. He's simply a true-blue friend to everyone in Mayberry.

HOWARD TAKES THE CAKE—*The county clerk checks out O.K. with Millie, the new worker at Boysinger's Bakery.*

Howard's a man with a mission as he plots his strategy at the courthouse:

GOOBER: Hey, look. She's going into Boysinger's Bakery.

ANDY: Oh, yeah. I bet she's gonna work there. Mr. Boysinger said he had a new girl coming in from Mt. Pilot.

HOWARD: Hey, Andy, when's the last time you had a cream bun?

ANDY: Ohhh…

HOWARD: Me, too, you know. And I got a real craving for a cream bun right now. How 'bout you?

ANDY: It's a little close to lunch, Howard.

HOWARD: Oh, it's my treat, Andy.

ANDY: Oh, I don't know.

HOWARD: Oh, come on, Andy. It's my treat, my treat.

ANDY: O.K. I wouldn't want to stand between you and a cream bun.

HOWARD: Oh, good! How 'bout you Goober?

GOOBER: I got to go to work, but you owe me one.

HOWARD: Right. Come on, Andy.

Over at the bakery, Howard puts his plan into action:

MILLIE: Well, what can I do for you?

HOWARD: Andy here has a real craving for a cream bun. Right, Andy?

ANDY: Yes, I do.

MILLIE: Oh, I'm sorry. Mr. Boysinger didn't bake the cream buns yet. What about a cinnamon roll or a ladyfinger? Oh, I know. What about a nice rum cake, sheriff?

ANDY: Oh, I don't know. It's a little early in the day for that.

HOWARD: Actually, the alcoholic content of rum cake is very negligible, Andy.

ANDY: Well, Howard, if you want to take your chances with rum cake, you're on your own. Well, I have to go to work. I'll see you, Millie.

MILLIE: Come again, sheriff.

ANDY: Hey, Howard, when you come out of here, you better be able to walk a chalk line.

Mr. Boysinger no doubt guards his recipe for cream buns pretty closely, but here's a recipe for bakery cinnamon buns.

Mr. Boysinger's Cinnamon Buns

1 envelope (¼ ounce) yeast
½ cup lukewarm water
1½ teaspoons sugar
½ cup milk
4 tablespoons shortening
⅓ cup sugar
¼ teaspoon salt
1 egg, beaten
4 cups all-purpose flour, sifted
¼ cup butter, melted
½ cup brown sugar
½ cup raisins
2 teaspoons ground cinnamon
1 cup confectioners' sugar

In a medium bowl, combine the yeast, water, and 1½ teaspoons of sugar. In a saucepan, scald the milk and add the shortening, ⅓ cup sugar, and salt. Allow to cool to lukewarm. Add the milk mixture and the egg to the yeast mixture. Stir in as much of the flour as needed to make a soft dough. Knead until smooth. Place in a bowl (greased with margarine) and cover with a cloth. Allow to rise in a warm place until the dough doubles in size (1 to 2 hours).

Briefly knead the dough on a floured surface. Roll out into a 10 x 18-inch rectangle. Spread the melted butter over top. Sprinkle with the brown sugar, raisins, and cinnamon. Roll up like a jelly roll. Cut the roll crosswise into pieces 1 inch wide. Place the pieces in a greased pan (about 9 inches square). Cover with a cloth, place in a warm place, and allow to double in size. Preheat the oven to 425°. Bake the buns for 20 to 25 minutes, or until golden brown. Meanwhile make a glaze by combining over medium-low heat the confectioners' sugar and enough water to make a spreadable frosting. Spread the glaze on the hot buns and serve immediately.
Makes 15 to 18 buns.

Smooth, Howard, smoooth:

MILLIE: Maybe you could tell me—where's a good place to eat?
HOWARD: Well, there's not much choice actually. Most of us eat at the Diner.
MILLIE: Well, if the Diner is good for most of you, it's good enough for me. Do I need a reservation?
HOWARD: Not if you go early. That's what I do. Maybe we could go early together.
MILLIE: Howard, I think that's very friendly.

Something tells us Goober has given food some thought from time to time:
GOOBER: Say, let me have one of them cinnamon buns. Seven cents, ain't they?
MILLIE: Right.
GOOBER: You know, Howard, less than a year ago—used to get 'em for six.
HOWARD: Yeah.
GOOBER: You don't have to put it in a box. I'll just eat it here. I don't like to eat on the street unless it's maybe an ice cream cone, apple, or peanuts.

Chocolate Rum Cake

1 box devil's food cake mix
1 small box (3½ ounces) instant chocolate
   pudding mix
4 eggs
½ cup sour cream
1 cup vegetable oil
½ cup dark rum
1 teaspoon vanilla extract
¼ teaspoon ground nutmeg
½ cup coffee
12 ounces semi-sweet chocolate chips
1 cup chopped pecans

Preheat the oven to 325°. Sift together the cake and pudding mixes. In a bowl combine the eggs, sour cream, oil, rum, vanilla, nutmeg, and coffee. Beat on low for 1 minute. Add the cake and pudding mixes, and beat on high speed for 2 minutes. Fold in the chocolate chips and nuts. Pour the batter into a greased and floured Bundt pan. Bake for 50 minutes and check for doneness. (Bake a little longer, if necessary, but do not overbake.) Let cool in the pan for 30 minutes. Remove from the pan and allow to cool completely on a wire rack. Wrap the cake to retain moisture. (It gets better if allowed to sit for a day or two.)
Serves 10 to 12.

Boysinger's Bakery

For fresh-baked goods in Mayberry, they don't come any fresher than Boysinger's Bakery on Main Street, just across from the courthouse. A cheery, striped awning out front over the sidewalk and the red-and-white checkered curtains on the windows invite customers to step right in.

The bakery is one of the friendliest places in town—thanks to the ever-congenial Millie Hutchins behind the counter. Goober says she's the sweetest thing in the shop, and it's for sure that Howard Sprague agrees. After all, that's where he proposed to her.

Once inside, customers can't help but notice shelves on the right that are groaning with delicious-looking loaves and buns of all types. And the counter on that side of the shop is where Millie operates the cash register, makes change, and weighs items on the scales.

Mr. Boysinger likes to offer a vast array of goodies—everything from wedding cakes (their specialty)—to bread, cakes, rolls, cream buns, and pastry, which are all baked fresh daily. Other sweet treats include cinnamon rolls, rum cake, ladyfingers, donuts, and Danish pastry. And, as an extra plus, the bakery uses "whole grain flour."

Boysinger's also offers real value and such deals as seven cents for a cinnamon bun and $1.25 for a chocolate layer cake (or just a buck if the cake is dented). Boysinger's Bakery offers such a warm atmosphere and alluring aromas that it's no wonder that Goober prefers to eat his purchases inside, which is convenient since he also doesn't like to eat on the street.

Opie Steps Up in Class

The real reason to cut back on those between-meal snacks:

AUNT BEE: Well, I'd better get supper ready.
OPIE: It's not supper, Aunt Bee.
AUNT BEE: It isn't?
OPIE: No, it's dinner. All the kids call supper, dinner. Supper is something you eat around eleven or twelve at night.
AUNT BEE: Well, we're not going to stay up that late to eat.

What they eat for lunch in ritzy Walnut Hills:
AUNT BEE: What'd they serve for lunch?
OPIE: Well, the first thing they served was an avocado salad…and a hot roast beef sandwich—not like the kind we have. This didn't have any fat or gristle.

Oh, yeah? Well, here's an everyday lunch in Mayberry. So there!:

AUNT BEE: All right, boys! Lunch is ready. Here, Billy, if you don't like the shrimp, why, you can have soup or you can have both, if you prefer.
BILLY: No, I'll just eat the shrimp.
AUNT BEE: Now we have the regular cocktail sauce or the lemon sauce, whichever you prefer.
OPIE: Or you can have both, if you prefer.
BILLY: I'll take the cocktail sauce, thank you. Gee, we never have shrimp for lunch, just every once in a while at dinner.
OPIE: Yeah, well.

Avocado and Black Bean Salad

2 small avocados
2 medium plum tomatoes
2 medium navel oranges
1 can (16 ounces) black beans, rinsed and drained
1 tablespoon chopped fresh cilantro or parsley
1 teaspoon salt
1 cup cubed Cheddar cheese
½ cup salsa

Cut each avocado in half; discard the pits. Peel the avocados. Cut the avocados and tomatoes into bite-sized chunks. Cut the peel and white pith from the oranges; discard. Cut each orange cross-wise into ¼-inch-thick slices. In a large bowl, with a rubber spatula, toss the avocados, tomatoes, oranges slices, and remaining ingredients to mix well.
Serves 6.

Poppy Seed Dressing for Avocado Salad

⅔ cup sugar
1 teaspoon dry mustard
1 teaspoon paprika
2 teaspoons poppy seeds
¼ teaspoon salt
⅓ cup honey

⅓ cup vinegar
1 tablespoon lemon juice
1 teaspoon grated onion
1 cup salad oil

Mix the first five ingredients in a large bowl. Then blend in the honey, vinegar, lemon juice, and onion. Add the oil in a slow stream, beating constantly with an electric mixer until thick. This is ideal for Avocado Salad, but is also excellent over grapefruit or other fresh fruit salads.
Makes 2 cups.

Walnut Hills Hot Roast Beef Sandwich

Leftover pot roast (*lean*)
White bread
Sliced cheese (*any kind, optional*)
Butter
Mustard

Cut the leftover meat into bite-sized pieces. Using 1 piece of bread, assemble meat and cheese according to taste (or appetite). Place 1 pat of butter onto a hot griddle. Place the assembled half of the sandwich onto the griddle. Spread mustard on the second piece of bread and place (mustard side down) on top of the open-faced sandwich. Carefully turn the sandwich over. Heat until golden brown on each side. Variation: Serve open faced with brown gravy.

Shrimp Cocktail with Lemon Sauce

1 package (8 ounces) shrimp
2 tablespoons lemon juice
¼ cup diced celery
1 package (6 ounces) slivered almonds
⅓ cup mayonnaise
1 tablespoon chili sauce
Pinch of dill weed

In a large saucepan, boil the shrimp until pink; then drain and add the lemon juice. Mix the other ingredients in a small bowl and add to the shrimp. Serve on a bed of lettuce.

Lemon Sauce:
3 tablespoons lemon juice
⅛ teaspoon dry mustard
1 bay leaf, crumbled

Combine all the ingredients in a small bowl and pour over the shrimp.
Serves 4.

Shrimp Cocktail Sauce

1 can (16 ounces) tomatoes
1 onion, peeled and quartered
1 teaspoon lemon juice
Lemon zest
2 ribs celery with leaves, chopped
2 sprigs thyme
2 sprigs parsley
1 bay leaf
1 tablespoon dried basil
1 carrot, diced
2 cloves
2 tablespoons butter, melted
2 tablespoons all-purpose flour
½ teaspoon sugar
1 teaspoon Worcestershire sauce

In a saucepan, boil the first 11 ingredients and then simmer for 20 to 30 minutes. Strain to remove the seeds, leaves, and big pieces of onion. In a separate saucepan over medium heat, combine the melted butter and flour. Add the tomato mixture, the sugar, and Worcestershire sauce. Simmer, while stirring constantly, for about 10 minutes. Serve with boiled, peeled, and deveined shrimp arranged on lettuce leaves in a cocktail dish or bowl and garnish with lemon wedges.
Makes about 1½ cups.

Duck on a Spit

1 duck (about 5 pounds)
1½ teaspoons salt
1 small onion
3 sprigs parsley

½ cup apple juice
½ cup corn syrup
1 tablespoon lemon juice

Wash the duck and pat dry. Rub the cavity with salt. Place the onion and parsley in the cavity. In a saucepan, combine the remaining ingredients and simmer for 15 to 20 minutes. Pin the neck skin of the duck back with a skewer. Flatten the wings over the breast and tie a string around the breast to hold the wings. Tie the drumsticks to the tail. Insert the spit rod through the center of the duck from the breast end toward the tail. Place the duck on the spit with holding forks. Settle the hot coals at the back of the firebox and place a drip pan under the spit area.

For the sauce, combine the apple juice, corn syrup, and lemon juice in a bowl. Using a baster, insert ¼ cup of the sauce into the cavity. Cook the duck for about 2 hours or until tender. Prick the skin often with a fork to let fat drain off. During the final 15 to 20 minutes of cooking, brush the duck with sauce every 5 minutes.
Serves 2.

Does the meal fit the bill?:

AUNT BEE: I hope you like duck, Billy.
BILLY: Duck?
OPIE: It's not the kind you shoot. It's the kind you buy at the store.

Aunt Bee and the Lecturer

Distinguished Chicken

2 chicken breasts
Salt and pepper, to taste
All-purpose flour
2 tablespoons butter
¼ pound fresh mushrooms, cleaned and sliced
½ teaspoon dried paprika
1 cup cream
2 egg yolks
2 slices country ham

Remove the skin from the chicken. Season with salt and pepper. Roll the breasts in flour and then brown in the butter in a skillet. Simmer until tender. Remove the chicken from the pan and add the mushrooms, paprika, and cream. Cook for 5 minutes and then blend in the egg yolks. In an iron skillet, fry the ham until good and tender. Serve the chicken over the ham and top with the sauce. (Triple the recipe to serve a party of 6, as when Professor St. John visited.)
Serves 2.

The rise and fall of a great chef:

AUNT BEE: Now, Opie, only one helping of chicken tonight. I cooked it in wine. And don't either of you slam any doors. I don't want my soufflé to fall.

OPIE: It fell last time and we didn't slam anything.

The soufflé must have fallen this time, too, because it never shows up at the dinner table.

Yeast Rolls

1 cup shortening
2 teaspoons salt
½ cup sugar
1 cup lukewarm water
2 eggs, beaten
2 packages (¼ ounce each) yeast dissolved in cold water
6 cups all-purpose flour, sifted

In a small bowl, mix the shortening, salt, and sugar; then add the lukewarm water. Add the eggs, yeast mixture, and flour; stir until mixed. Put in the refrigerator until ready to use. When ready to bake, preheat the oven to 425°, shape the dough into rolls, and place on a greased baking sheet or greased muffin tin. Bake for 15 to 18 minutes.
Makes enough dough for 36 rolls.

Green Onions

4 bunches green onions
3 tablespoons butter
1 teaspoon salt
1 cup boiling water
½ cup melted butter
Pepper, to taste

Wash the onions and cut the stems to about finger length. Place them in a saucepan with the 3 tablespoons of butter, salt, and water. Cover and cook for about 5 minutes over medium heat. Drain well. Place in a small serving dish and pour the melted butter over top. Sprinkle with pepper and serve.
Serves 4.

Glazed Carrots

6 carrots
1 cup brown sugar
¾ cup melted butter
¼ teaspoon ground nutmeg
½ teaspoon ground cinnamon

Preheat the oven to 350°. Trim, scrape, and rinse the carrots. Cut the carrots lengthwise into ½-inch wide strips about 3 inches in length. Place side by side in a baking dish and cover with brown sugar. Top with the melted butter. Sprinkle with nutmeg and cinnamon. Bake until the carrots are glazed and tender. (As the brown sugar and butter begin to form a sauce, you can baste the carrots to promote thorough glazing.) Serve topped with a spoonful of sauce per serving.
Serves 4.

Homemade Blackberry Jam

Blackberries
Sugar
Lemon juice
Vanilla extract

Wash the blackberries and place them in a saucepan. Bring to a slow boil with just enough water to barely cover the bottom of the pan. Boil for 5 minutes. For every cup of pulp produced, add ¾ cup sugar, 1 teaspoon of lemon juice, and 3 drops of vanilla. Stir the mixture until the sugar dissolves; then boil until the mixture thickens, about 15 to 20 minutes, depending on the quantity of blackberries. (Overcooking will damage the texture and flavor.) Pour the jam into sterilized jars and, when cooled, seal with paraffin.

Nesselrode Pie

4 teaspoons unflavored gelatin
½ cup sugar
¼ cup cornstarch
½ teaspoon salt
3 cups milk
6 egg yolks, slightly beaten
1 bar (4 ounces) sweet cooking chocolate, grated
1 teaspoon vanilla extract
½ teaspoon rum flavoring
1 jar (10 ounces) Nesselrode
3 cups chilled whipping cream, divided
1 nine-inch pie crust, baked

In a pan, mix the gelatin, sugar, cornstarch, salt, milk, and egg yolks. Cook over medium heat while stirring constantly until the mixture thickens. Boil and stir for 1 more minute. Pour 1½ cups of the hot mixture into a bowl and set aside to cool.

Save 2 tablespoons of grated chocolate for topping, and blend the remaining chocolate and vanilla into the hot mixture prepared above. Cool completely.

Line a 9-inch pie pan with waxed paper. Stir the rum flavoring and Nesselrode into the 1½ cup mixture cooled in bowl. In a chilled bowl, beat 2 cups of whipping cream until stiff. Fold half of the whipped cream into each mixture. Pour the chocolate mixture into the baked pie shell. Pour the Nesselrode mixture into the waxed paper-lined pan. Chill each until firm. Loosen the edge of Nesselrode layer and invert on the chocolate filling. In a chilled bowl, beat the remaining cream until stiff. Spread over the pie, covering completely, and sprinkle with the reserved chocolate gratings. Serve immediately.
Serves 6 to 8.

SWEET PROPOSAL—*If Opie would ever get out of there with that chocolate cake, Howard and Millie just might get engaged.*

It's "Next Stop Budgetville" when Andy and Helen join Howard and Millie on the train trip to West Virginia for Howard and Millie's wedding. And there's about to be some wheeling and dealing:

HOWARD: What do you say we go on down and put on the feedbag?

ANDY: Lead the way…

ANDY: Now listen, Howard, I think I oughta take care of Helen's and my part.

HOWARD: Your money's no good here, soldier. I'll take care of everything.

ANDY: Well, that's nice of you, Howard.

HOWARD: Ah-ah. Forget it.

ANDY: Well.

HOWARD: Gosh, you know it's been a long time since I been in one of these dining cars.

ANDY: Me too.

HOWARD: (*Looking in disbelief at the prices on the menu*) Things have changed a little. I mean the prices.

ANDY: Yeah, well, like everything.

ANDY: You know what I might have? The special—fish cakes—might just hit the spot.

HOWARD: Know something, Andy. I had my eye on that baby too.

ANDY: Did you really?

HOWARD: Yeah. You know what I like about fish? It combines the high nutritional value with flavor at a modest price.

ANDY: You can't ask much more of a fish than that, can you?

HOWARD: Anything to start with?

ANDY: Oh, I don't know. Maybe a roll.

HOWARD: Well, we certainly have the same tastes. I'm a roll man myself.

ANDY: Well, good.

Train Rolls

4 cups all-purpose flour, divided
½ teaspoon baking soda
2 envelopes (¼ ounce each) dry yeast
1¼ cups buttermilk
3 tablespoons sugar
½ cup water
1 teaspoon salt
½ cup shortening

In a large bowl, combine 1½ cups of the flour with the yeast, sugar, salt, and baking soda. Mix thoroughly. In a saucepan, heat the buttermilk, water, and shortening over medium heat until warm. Add to the flour/yeast mixture and blend at medium speed for 4 to 5 minutes. Work in the remaining flour (more or less) to form a solid dough. Knead on a floured surface until the dough is a uniform texture and elastic.

Place the dough in a bowl and lightly grease the top. Cover and let rise in a warm place (a warmed oven turned off works well) until the dough doubles in size (about 1 hour). Punch the dough down and then form into about two dozen balls. Place, well spaced apart, on a greased cookie sheet. Cover again and place in a warm place to double in size. Preheat the oven to 400°. Bake the rolls for about 15 minutes or until golden brown. Brush with butter. They're ready to serve, or they can be cooled on racks. (They freeze well too, but they're never better than hot out of the oven!)
Makes about 2 dozen.

This train is about to be derailed:

MILLIE: Here we are.
HELEN: Now, we weren't too long, were we?
HOWARD: It's always too long when I'm away from Millie.
MILLIE: Oh, Howard, you're sweet.
HOWARD: We've already decided.
ANDY: We're having the special—fish cakes.
HELEN: Oh, well, I think I'll have fish cakes too.
ANDY: We figured we'd start off with a roll.
HELEN: Oh, fine, fine.
HOWARD: How about you, dear?
MILLIE: Oh, that all sounds so dull. Let's see. I'll have the shrimp cocktail, and Porterhouse steak with au gratin potatoes and celery hearts and probably fudge layer cake. I'll see. Is there anything wrong, dear?

Howard is speechless and shakes his head no.
For Shrimp Cocktail like Millie's, see the recipe on page 187.

Priced-Right Fish Cakes

2 cans (6 ounces each) tuna
1 large egg, beaten
½ cup cracker crumbs

Onions and green pepper, chopped fine (*optional*)
Oil

Form ingredients into patties and fry in oil. (A slice of cheese melted on top makes a delicious sandwich on a bun.)
Serves 2.

REALLY ON A ROLL— *Howard keeps his expenses on track when ordering on the train.*

Porterhouse Steak

½ to 1-pound steak per person
Pepper
Steak spice
Garlic
Barbecue sauce, optional

Brown each side of the steak for about 5 minutes; sprinkle with pepper, steak spice, and garlic. For medium well, grill about 25 minutes. At the last flip of each steak, brush on barbecue sauce if desired.

Au Gratin Potatoes

4 cups diced boiled potatoes
½ cup cream
Salt and pepper, to taste
½ cup grated Cheddar cheese
Bread crumbs
Paprika

Preheat the oven to 350°. In a large bowl, mix together the potatoes, cream, and salt and pepper. Place in a greased casserole and top with the cheese and some bread crumbs and paprika. Heat until golden brown.
Serves 4.

Fudge Layer Cake

Cake:
2 cups sugar
1¾ cups all-purpose flour
1½ teaspoons baking powder
1½ teaspoons baking soda
1 cup cocoa
1 teaspoon salt
2 eggs
1 cup milk
⅔ cup vegetable oil
2 teaspoons vanilla extract
1 cup boiling water

Preheat the oven to 350°. In a large bowl, mix the dry ingredients. Add the eggs, milk, oil, and vanilla. Beat on medium speed for 3 to 4 minutes. Add the boiling water. Pour into two greased and floured 9-inch pans. Bake for 30 minutes. Let cool for 15 minutes and then remove to wire racks to cool completely. Frost and serve.

Frosting:
½ cup butter, melted
1 cup cocoa
3 cups confectioners' sugar
½ cup milk
1½ teaspoons vanilla extract

In a large bowl, combine the butter and cocoa. Add the confectioners' sugar, milk, and vanilla. Beat the mixture on medium speed until spreadable.
Serves 10.

NO MAN IS AN ISLAND—*When Howard Sprague follows his rainbow to St. Benedict's Island in the Caribbean, he surely gets his fill of fish, such as the ones that island native Sebastian is carrying here. Howard eventually returns to Mayberry, of course, and says, "I guess I just followed my rainbow to the wrong end. My pot of gold is right here in Mayberry."*

Sebastian's Fish St. Benedict

2 pounds fish fillets (at least ¾-inch thick)
Lime juice
Salt and pepper, to taste
1 garlic clove, minced
2 sprigs rosemary
6 tablespoons olive oil
Almond slices
1 tablespoon butter

Preheat the oven to 450°. Arrange the fillets in a shallow baking dish. Sprinkle the lime juice and salt and pepper over the fish. In a separate bowl, combine the garlic, rosemary, and oil, and then brush over the fillets. Bake for 20 to 25 minutes, being careful not to overcook. (The fish should be moist and flaky.) Baste with the drippings every 5 minutes or so. While the fish is cooking, sauté the almonds in butter. Top the fish with the almonds just before serving.
Serves 4.

Emmett's Brother-in-Law

NOT MUCH LAYS ON HIS CHEST—*Goober digs right into Martha Clark's special dip.*

Corned Beef Potato Salad

4 cups cubed cooked potatoes
1 can (12 ounces) corned beef, cubed
½ dill pickle, diced
½ cup chopped celery
¼ cup chopped onion
¼ cup salad oil
1 tablespoon vinegar
½ teaspoon salt
¼ teaspoon garlic powder
¼ teaspoon freshly ground pepper
⅔ cup sour cream or low-fat sour cream
Crisp lettuce
Cherry tomatoes

In a large bowl, toss the potatoes, corned beef, pickle, celery, and onion. In a covered jar, shake the oil, vinegar, salt, garlic powder, and pepper. Pour over the corned beef mixture and toss. Cover and refrigerate for 2 hours or longer. Just prior to serving, mix in the sour cream and toss. Season to taste. Serve on lettuce and garnish with tomatoes.
Serves 4 to 6.

Martha's Mexican Chip Dip

1 pound ground beef
Chopped onions
2 cans (15 ounces each) jalapeño bean dip or refried beans
1 can (14½ ounces) diced tomatoes
1½ pounds of Velveeta cheese, cubed

Brown the beef and onions in a large saucepan. Add the bean dip or refried beans and diced tomatoes. Simmer until the juice is gone (about 30 minutes). Add the cheese and melt. Serve with chips. (This may be frozen and put in a baking dish and reheated.)

The Mayberry Chef

The owner of the Siler City TV station is looking for the perfect host for his new cooking show:

MR. PHILLIPS: In our search, we discovered that Miss Taylor had innumerable recipes of her own published in local papers and has consistently won prizes in county fairs.

ANDY: Oh, yeah. She's been a winner all right.

AUNT BEE: (*Entering the room*) Who ever heard of not cutting off some of the fat off of pot roast before weighing it? I've been buying pot roasts for over forty years and not once, not once, has any butcher ever refused to cut off at least some of the fat.

TV dinners:

ANDY: How is it?

OPIE: Fine. What is it?

ANDY: Corned beef hash.

OPIE: That's what I thought.

ANDY: Opie, we can keep going around like this or you can tell me what's wrong.

OPIE: Food, Pa, food!

ANDY: Well, you're getting plenty to eat.

OPIE: Yeah, not that there's anything wrong with your cooking. I mean, I know that it's all nutritious and everything, but...

ANDY: But what?

OPIE: Couldn't we go out to the Diner one night. I'll pay for it!

WATCHING WHAT THEY'RE NOT EATING—*Opie and Andy watch Aunt Bee's cooking show while surviving on Andy's home cooking.*

AUNT BEE: *(On TV)* Now I've always felt that food that looks good tastes good, and when a man comes home from work he likes to see an attractive meal and a well-set table.

Corned Beef Hash

2 cups chopped cooked corned or roast beef
2 cups chopped cooked potatoes
⅔ cup chopped onion
½ teaspoon salt
Pinch of pepper
¼ cup shortening
⅔ cup water

Combine the corned beef, potatoes, onion, salt, and pepper. Melt the shortening in a large skillet and spread the meat mixture in skillet. Brown for 10 to 15 minutes, stirring often. Stir in the water, cover, reduce the heat, and cook 10 minutes longer.
Serves 2.

Mrs. Parkins's Tuna Salad

2 cans (6 ounces each) water-packed tuna, drained
4 hard-boiled eggs, grated
3 ribs celery, finely chopped
½ cup chopped pecans
½ cup diced dill pickle
1 large apple, diced
Mayonnaise

In a large bowl, mix all of the ingredients and salt lightly. Mix in enough mayonnaise to hold together.
Serves 2 to 4.

One of Aunt Bee's World Famous Rib Roasts

½ cup olive oil
4- to 5-pound rib roast
2 tablespoons vinegar
2 tablespoons mustard
3 tablespoons all-purpose flour
Potatoes
Carrots
Onions
1 cup water
Salt and pepper to taste

Heat the oil in a skillet and brown the roast a bit on both sides. Then take the roast out and put it in a baking dish. Preheat the oven to 400°. Splash 2 tablespoons of vinegar over the roast. Next apply the mustard and the flour by rubbing the flour into the mustard. Place the potatoes, carrots, and onions around the roast, add the cup of water, cover, and cook until you smell the roast (about 30 minutes). Then turn down the oven to 350° and cook for 3 more hours.
Serves about 8.

AUNT BEE: (*To Andy and Opie*): Now you two go on up and get washed and in twenty minutes you'll have one of my world-famous rib roasts.

Chicken in a Pot

1 pound boneless chicken breasts
1 can (10¾ ounces) cream of mushroom soup
¼ cup white wine (*optional*)
¼ teaspoon pepper
¼ teaspoon chopped capers
1 cup grated Provolone or Swiss cheese
1½ cups dry herbed stuffing mix
⅓ cup melted butter

Preheat the oven to 350°. Grease a round casserole. Cut the chicken into strips. In a bowl, mix the soup, wine, pepper, and capers. Layer half of the chicken strips in the bottom of the casserole. Cover that chicken with half of the cheese and then half of the soup mixture. Layer the rest of the chicken, then the rest of the cheese and soup mixture. Top with the stuffing mix. Pour the melted butter over all. Bake for 45 minutes to 1 hour.
Serves 4.

TRICKY TREAT—*Aunt Bee serves up her delicious homemade pumpkin pie as part of her attempt to steer Andy's vote toward using church money for new choir robes.*

One of Andy's Favorites (Roast Beef)

4 pounds rib roast
3 tablespoons vegetable oil
2 onions, sliced
1 can (20 ounces) tomato juice
1 teaspoon cloves
1 tablespoon Worcestershire sauce
1 teaspoon ground cinnamon
1 teaspoon salt
2 teaspoons pepper

Rub the roast with the oil and brown in a roasting pan. Combine the remaining ingredients in a large bowl and pour over the roast. Bring the mixture to a boil and then simmer, basting occasionally, for about 5 hours, or until the meat crumbles. Serve with the gravy from the pan.
Serves 10 to 12.

Pumpkin Pie

2 eggs
1 can (16 ounces) pumpkin
¾ cup sugar
½ teaspoon salt
1 teaspoon ground cinnamon
½ teaspoon ground ginger
¼ teaspoon cloves
1⅔ cups evaporated milk
1 nine-inch unbaked pie crust

Preheat the oven to 375°. Mix together the first eight ingredients in a large bowl. Pour into the pie crust. Bake for 1 hour. Serve with ice cream.
Serves 6 to 8.

---

*S*inging praises for Aunt Bee's cooking:

OPIE: Boy, that was real good.
ANDY: Yeah, it was real good.
OPIE: Roast beef's one of your favorites, isn't it, Pa?
ANDY: Yeah, she had all my favorites. 'Bout all we need now to have a perfect meal is pumpkin pie à la mode.
AUNT BEE: (*Entering room*) And for dessert—pumpkin pie à la mode. There we are.
OPIE: Is this what we call lobbying, Pa?
ANDY: If you mean, is she working on me for the choir robes? I'd say yes.

Barney Hosts a Summit Meeting

WORKER BEE—*Mayberry is all abuzz when the Taylors host a summit meeting at their house. On short notice, Aunt Bee hurriedly prepares sandwiches for the diplomats' first snack.*

IT'S A RAID!— *"This is what we call in America, raiding the icebox."*—Mr. Clifford, the American diplomat

Tuna Pita Sandwiches

½ cup margarine
½ cup all-purpose flour
1 tablespoon dry Italian salad dressing mix
2 cups milk
1 cup shredded Provolone cheese

1 cup sliced ripe olives
1 cup green pepper strips
2 cans (6 ounces each) tuna, drained
Pita pockets

Make a thick sauce in a saucepan over medium heat of margarine, flour, dressing mix, and milk. Add the cheese and stir until melted. Add the olives, pepper strips, and tuna. Heat and serve in pita pockets. *Makes enough for 6 to 8 pockets.*

Potato Salad

6 medium potatoes, diced
1 rib celery, chopped
1 carrot, chopped
1 sweet pepper, chopped
4 or 5 small sweet pickles, chopped

1 small onion, chopped
4 tablespoons of Miracle Whip
1 tablespoon mustard
½ teaspoon celery seed (*optional*)
Paprika to taste

Cook the potatoes. Drain and let cool. Add the celery, carrot, sweet pepper, pickles, and onion to the potatoes. Mix with the salad dressing, mustard, and celery seed. Sprinkle paprika on top for garnish.
Serves 4 to 6.

Summit Meeting Meat Loaf

It's tops!

1½ pounds ground beef
1 cup cracker crumbs
2 eggs, beaten
1 can (6 ounces) tomato paste
½ cup finely chopped onion

2 tablespoons chopped green pepper
1½ tablespoons salt
Dash thyme
Bacon strips

Preheat the oven to 350°. In a large bowl, combine the first eight ingredients and mix well. Shape into a loaf in a baking dish. Place bacon strips on the summit of the loaf. Bake for about 1 hour.
Serves 4 to 6.

Bee's Bread Pudding

2 cups white bread crusts
½ cup sugar
½ cup brown sugar
2 eggs
1 cup milk
½ teaspoon ground cinnamon
1 teaspoon vanilla extract
¼ teaspoon salt
½ cup butter, melted
Raisins (*optional*)

Combine the bread and sugars in a large mixing bowl. In a blender, combine the eggs, milk, cinnamon, vanilla, and salt. Blend until it froths. Pour over the bread and sugar mixture and let stand for 1 to 2 hours.

Preheat the oven to 350°. Add the butter (and raisins) and mix thoroughly. Pour into a 9 x 13-inch baking dish or cake pan and bake for 25 minutes. Top with sauce.

Sauce:
½ cup butter
1 cup sugar
1 egg, beaten
¼ cup Otis's favorite bourbon

In the top of a double boiler, melt the butter and sugar. Gradually add the egg while stirring with a whisk. Cool a little and then add the whiskey. Pour the sauce over the pudding. Note: If you're not planning to serve all of the pudding at once, pour the sauce on each individual serving; then refrigerate and reheat the pudding and the sauce separately. *Serves 6.*

---

*S*ummit meeting minutes:

"I thought I heard something down here in the kitchen. Aw, you're hungry, you poor things."
    —*Aunt Bee*
"You sit right down. My mother always said if you eat standing up, it goes right to your legs."
    —*Aunt Bee*
"Let's see what we have here...Some potato salad. There you are. Meat loaf and bread pudding."
    —*Aunt Bee*
"If I'd have known there was going to be a summit meeting in my kitchen, I would have washed the floor."
    —*Aunt Bee*
"So, my congratulations to whoever it was that steered us here...to a quiet informal meeting in a homey kitchen with a charming, charming hostess."
    —*Mr. Clifford*

The Wedding

PILLOW TALK— *Howard's first party at his swinging, new bachelor pad is almost more than his fellow Mayberrians can bear—that is, until Emmett arrives and fixes things by really cutting a rug.*

Timing like a Swiss watch:

HOWARD: Well, let's get the old show on the road, eh? How's about a Swiss cheese sandwich?
ANDY: Uh, gee, Howard, they look awfully good, but we just ate an hour ago.
HOWARD: Goob?
GOOBER: Naw, I'd like to finish my drink.
HOWARD: Oh, well, why don't we make ourselves comfy, huh? Helen, why don't you just sit down right here on this nice pretty red pillow. There you are. Andy, make yourself comfortable right there. There you are. I'll just plunk down right here on this purple pillow.

Wedding Bells Rice Pudding

½ cup rice
1½ cups water
½ teaspoon salt
¼ cup margarine

1 cup milk
½ cup sugar
Ground nutmeg or cinnamon (*optional*)

Cook the rice in the water with the salt in a double boiler. When nearly done, add the remaining ingredients. Mix well. Allow to set. It's then ready to serve—either warmed or chilled.
Serves 4.

Swiss Cheese Sandwiches for a Party

24 long slices Swiss cheese
Mayonnaise

24 slices white bread

Cut the slices of Swiss cheese in half to give you 48 sandwich-sized slices. Spread mayonnaise on one side of every piece of bread. Place a half slice of cheese on each mayonnaised surface. Spread more mayonnaise on half of the cheese slices and make sandwiches by matching them with the pieces of Swiss that don't have mayonnaise on them. Then you just cut the sandwiches in half and put toothpicks in them. It's that simple. But no matter how you spread it on or how you slice it, you'll have a tough time finding any takers. Oh, well. They're still good.
Makes 12 sandwiches.

Sam for Town Council

PIE IN THE FACE—*Once the town council election is over, Aunt Bee begins her campaign to win Sam's favor.*

Election Night Lemon Meringue Pie

1 cup sugar
3 tablespoons cornstarch
1½ cups cold water
3 egg yolks, slightly beaten
Zest from 1 lemon
¼ cup lemon juice
1 tablespoon butter
1 9-inch baked pie crust

Preheat the oven to 350°. In a large saucepan over medium heat, combine the sugar and cornstarch. Gradually stir in the water until the mixture is smooth. Add the egg yolks. Bring the mixture to a boil while stirring constantly. Boil for 1 minute and then remove from the heat. Add the lemon zest, lemon juice, and butter. Stir to mix and then allow to cool. Pour into the pie crust, top with meringue, and bake for 15 minutes, or until lightly browned.

Meringue:
3 egg whites
¼ teaspoon cream of tartar
6 tablespoons sugar

In a mixing bowl beat the egg whites and cream of tartar at high speed with an electric mixer until frothy. Gradually add the sugar, beating well with each addition. Continue beating at high speed until the sugar is gone and stiff peaks form.
Serves 6 to 8.

Andy and Opie, Housekeepers

AFTER ALL THE COOKING AND EATING—*Don't forget…there's the dishwashing to do…but "not with your* sleeve!"

Mayberry TV Dinners

Members of *The Andy Griffith Show* Rerun Watchers Club often find inspiration for their chapter names in the food and beverage of Mayberry. More than fifty of these culinary names were listed in either *Aunt Bee's Mayberry Cookbook* or *Aunt Bee's Delightful Desserts*. Here are sixteen recent names reflecting a strong appetite for Mayberry:

"Drink Hard Cider and Holler 'Flinch'"	Ramseur, NC
"Bread!"	Savannah, GA
"What You Need Is More Sauce!"	Haines, AK
"I Don't Chew My Cabbage Twice"	Phillipsburg, NJ
Bendlemight's Porchside Cider Sippers	Nickel Ranch, CA
"This Cider's Turned Hard"	Conyers, GA/Calumet City, IL
"Pearly Onions Twang My Buds"	Leavenworth, KS
"Barney, You're Gassed!"	Cedarsburg, WI
The Mayberry Donut Shop	Cyberspace
Mr. Cookie Bar	Aiken, SC
"'Bout to Pop"	Grayson, GA
Tomato Catchers Club	Lecanto, FL
"Bad Old Home Pickles"	Kingston Springs, TN
Morrison Sisters Elixir	Eden, NC
"Food and Water for My Men and Horses!"	Hokes Bluff, AL
"I Came to Fill My Vase"	Waxhaw, NC

Somebody's always in the kitchen in Mayberry. To find out more, write *The Andy Griffith Show* Rerun Watchers Club at:

TAGSRWC
9 Music Square South
Suite 146
Nashville, TN 37203-3203

Index